I Believe

James Forsyth

I Believe

The Creed and You

NOVALIS

© 2012 Novalis Publishing Inc.

Cover: Blaine Herrmann
Layout: Audrey Wells

Published by Novalis

Publishing Office
10 Lower Spadina Avenue, Suite 400
Toronto, Ontario, Canada
M5V 2Z2

Head Office
4475 Frontenac Street
Montréal, Québec, Canada
H2H 2S2

www.novalis.ca

Library and Archives Canada Cataloguing in Publication

Forsyth, James, 1930-
    I believe : the Creed and you / James Forsyth.

Issued also in an electronic format.
ISBN 978-2-89646-469-2

    1. Apostles' Creed. I. Title.

BT993.3.F67 2012   238'.11   C2012-903871-7

Printed in Canada.

We acknowledge the financial support of the Government of Canada through
the Canada Book Fund for business development activities.

5   4   3   2   1   16   15   14   13   12

Contents

Man lives on truth and on being loved:
on being loved by the truth.
He needs God, the God who draws close to him,
interprets for him the meaning of life,
and thus points him toward the path of life.

—Pope Benedict XVI

Introduction

This book is addressed to Catholic Christians; its aim is to explore the meaning of our Christian faith by reflecting on the articles (statements of belief) contained in the Apostles' Creed. It is called the Apostles' Creed because, in the early Church and even into the Middle Ages, there was a belief that it was composed by the twelve apostles at Pentecost when they received the Holy Spirit. Though most scholars no longer take this view, the Creed still bears that title because it is a general statement of faith that is seen to truly reflect the beliefs of the apostles and the early Christians.

When Arius, a priest of Alexandria in Egypt, taught that God the Son was not divine but a creation of God the Father to be the instrument of the Father's activity in the world, Church leaders had to debate the question and respond. In the year 325, the Church therefore convoked the Council of Nicaea, which condemned Arianism and confirmed the divinity of the Son as "begotten, not made" of the Father. The word the Council used to describe the Son's sharing of the divine nature with the Father was the

Greek word *homoousios*, that is, "one in being" or – as we now say at Mass – "consubstantial" with the Father.

Because of resistance to this term in some quarters, the Council of Constantinople was convoked in 381. This Council reaffirmed the Nicene formula on the divine nature of Christ. In this way, the Nicene Creed – the official statement of Christian belief issued by the Council of Nicaea – has survived to this day and is the Creed we now recite at Sunday Mass for most of the Church year.

As the source for this discussion of Catholic doctrine I have chosen the Apostles' Creed rather than the Nicene Creed for the following reasons: (1) it is more ancient; (2) it is not a response to doctrinal disputes, which belong to an era of Church history and are of little concern to today's average Catholic; and (3) it is a statement of faith with which the average Catholic is more familiar – it is the Creed we learned as children; and it is the form of the Creed used as a profession of faith in the ritual of baptism, in the Easter liturgy and in the recitation of the rosary.

In the early Church, the Apostles' Creed was recited by the catechumens – those preparing to be baptized – as their "profession of faith." It is still used today in the form of three questions addressed to those who are being baptized. They are asked to affirm their belief in what the Creed says about God the Father, God the Son who became man (Christ), and God the Holy Spirit. (In the case of infant baptism, the sponsors reply.) The same three questions are addressed to the faithful in the Easter liturgy, when they renew their baptismal promises. The Creed is divided into these three parts, which correspond to the three Persons of the Trinity and to the formula of baptism: "I baptize you in the name of the Father and of the Son and of the Holy Spirit."

In writing this commentary on the Apostles' Creed, I am conscious that reciting the Creed – or any other formal prayer – can become a mechanical exercise in which we often pay little attention to what we are saying. Perhaps this is because we understand the words as abstract formulas referring to ideas or concepts that have little relevance or meaning for our day-to-day lives. And yet the Creed is meant to have a personal meaning for each of us. This is because it has some important things to say to us and about us. In other words, the Creed has a *human* meaning. It speaks *to* us about God, the Trinity, Christ, the Holy Spirit, and more, but, in doing so, it says something *about* us. I believe that only when we understand the Creed in this way can we say it with attention and conviction. Only when I understand and accept what the Creed says about me can the Creed become not just the teachings of the Church but my own personal beliefs and convictions – my personal creed.

In this book we will make our way through the Creed with an emphasis on this personal meaning. We shall try to discover the meaning of the Creed not only in abstract theological terms, but of its meaning for our human lives. In studying the Creed in this way, we shall make use of two guiding principles that are long-standing features of Catholic thought:

1. Thomas Aquinas' idea of the *reciprocal relationship between human nature and divine grace.* In simple terms, this means that (a) the more fully human we become, the better equipped we are to respond to the grace of God or, as Aquinas put it, *grace presupposes nature*; and (b) the more we respond to the grace of God, the more fully human we become or, as Aquinas put it, *grace perfects nature.*

2. The principle of the *analogy of being* between the human and the divine. This means we can understand something about God by examining our human life and experience. An analogy helps us understand a difficult concept without explaining it fully. If one thing is *analogous* to another, it is partly the same and partly different. For example, the human understanding of fatherhood can tell us something about the fatherhood of God. And if the word "salvation" means "healing," then the human meaning of healing can give us some understanding of salvation. In this way, something that is beyond our human capacity to understand can be rendered humanly meaningful.

I suggest that we look at the articles of the Creed in terms of what our faith means for our human existence – not as something "tacked on" to our humanity, but as corresponding to our deepest human desires. This is what I mean by the "human meaning" of our faith. To explore this human meaning, we must go through the Creed slowly and reflect on the meaning of each article of faith and its relevance for our human existence. Let's begin.

1

Belief

I believe, therefore I am a somebody.

What is a "somebody"?

In the 17th century, the French philosopher René Descartes began his search for truth by doubting everything he thought he knew – even his own existence. But the fact that he was thinking about the question convinced him that he existed as a thinking being. In a statement that has become famous, he concluded, "I think, therefore I am." (Since Descartes wrote in both French and Latin, it appears as *Je pense, donc je suis*, but it became more famous in its Latin form, *Cogito ergo sum*.) If you are wondering what this has to do with the Creed, I want to suggest to you that if you can say the Apostles' Creed with real faith and conviction – that is, if you can say it in such a way that it becomes a statement of your own personal beliefs and not just an empty formula – then it becomes a statement of who you are, because it states what you personally stand for. My beliefs help to define what kind of person I am. They make me a somebody. I can thus go a step further than Descartes and say, I believe, therefore I am a somebody.

In our present context, growing up can be seen as a process of becoming that unique somebody I potentially am – that unique person who is different from everyone else, the somebody I was meant to be. In the process of growing up, that somebody is gradually revealed. One problem that all of us, especially as teenagers, encounter is that this need to become a unique somebody must compete with its opposite – the need to be accepted and to fit in. This pressures me to be like everyone else, or at least everyone in my age, social or occupational group. In fact, this conflict between individuality and conformity seems to be a lifelong experience.

And yet both these needs are important. Neither can be sacrificed. With too much conformity – too much trying to be like everyone else – the unique somebody I am meant to be gets lost. Peter Maurin, co-founder with Dorothy Day of the Catholic Worker movement, once described a conformist as "someone who tries to be a somebody by being like everybody which makes him a nobody."[1] On the other hand, too much trying to be different from everyone else cuts me off from other people, and the whole social side of life gets lost. It's all very well to want to become a unique somebody, but I need to be connected to other people to be unique. I need other people to help me find myself. When I have done so, that unique somebody I have become needs

---

[1] Peter Maurin, *Easy Essays* (Eugene, OR: Wipf and Stock, 2006), 90.

to fit in and play a role in the lives of other people, which I can't do if I am too preoccupied with myself. So whether I try too hard to be different from everyone else or try too hard to be like everyone else, in either case it becomes a self-defeating exercise.

How do we manage to avoid these two extremes? If the process of growing up follows the normal pattern, I discover certain things about myself that distinguish me or set me apart from others while, at the same time, not cutting me off completely from them. It all begins in infancy. As infants, we come to some kind of primitive awareness that we are a separate person from our mother. So the first separation we experience is that of self and mother. We took the first step towards becoming a unique somebody; that process of growing away from dependence on mother and becoming independent continued over the years.

But while we are becoming increasingly independent of mother, something else is going on. The need for independence does not cause us to reject mother, but to develop a closer relationship with her. So we strike a balance, holding on to mother while at the same time asserting our independence from her. As toddlers we set off to do things on our own, but go running to mother if things didn't go well. And this is how it goes throughout life. Becoming a unique somebody does not mean we no longer need other people. This is also true of our sexual identity. When we discover that we are a boy or girl, we do not reject the opposite sex any more than we reject our mother when we assert ourselves as separate individuals.

Somewhere between the ages of four and six, we make another separation or distinction. We begin to distinguish right from wrong, good from evil. As we develop a moral sense – a conscience – we try to identify with the good and reject evil, to choose what is right and avoid what is wrong. At first, of course, we still think of good and bad in terms of what is "allowed" and "not allowed" by our parents. (e.g., I'm allowed to watch TV but not allowed to watch certain shows.) As our conscience matures, however, we begin to understand that some ways of behaving are good and right while others are bad and wrong, apart from whether they are allowed or not. Some things are to be done because they are good in themselves, while others are to be avoided because they are bad or evil in themselves. Here we are telling ourselves what was allowed or not allowed, rather than relying on our parents. Psychologists call this introjection or internalizing. This means we are truly beginning to develop a conscience. It also means that the somebody we are trying to become now has a moral quality and knows right from wrong. We are beginning to stand for something and against something else.

But is it enough to simply choose what is good and reject what is evil? In the same way that becoming independent does not mean rejecting our mother, choosing good over evil does not mean rejecting the part of us that wants to choose evil. This aspect of ourselves that wants to be mean or vindictive or dishonest or selfish is still part of us, and we cannot pretend otherwise. We do not have to give into it willingly or be preoccupied with it. We simply must have a healthy awareness of it. When we experience the sacrament of reconciliation, we do not confess our sins to get rid of that "dark side." Confession means admitting that this aspect is part of us and asking forgiveness for having surrendered to it. But it follows that this approach involves a certain acceptance of that not-so-nice side. Not accepting it or pretending it doesn't exist causes us the most trouble. Whether we confess our moral failings directly to God or in the sacrament of reconciliation, the result is not self-rejection but self-acceptance based on God's acceptance and forgiveness of us – dark side and all. If God accepts us the way we are, then trying to be good does not involve rejecting any aspect of ourselves.

Becoming a unique somebody, then, is a matter of acquiring a personal identity. So far we have seen three building blocks of that identity: individual identity, sexual identity and moral identity. Each of these begins with a child discovering he or she is one thing and not another: an individual separate from mother; a boy/girl not a girl/ boy; someone who wants to be good, not bad. Nevertheless mother, girl/boy and dark side cannot be eliminated. I need them to be who I am. In short, these three types of identity combine to create an individual male or female with a conscience.

How does belief make me a somebody?

There is more, however, to being a somebody than being an individual male or female with a conscience. When we reached puberty, something else started to happen. The old certainties of childhood began to fade. The distinction between right and wrong was no longer so clear-cut. The result of beginning to think about things and have opinions is uncertainty. As we grow older and acquire more knowledge and experience, we develop a mindset, an outlook, a set of assumptions or opinions about how things are and how things ought to be. Apart from the physical changes of puberty, an intellectual development is going on. The goal of this development is to acquire not only knowledge but also a set of deep-seated beliefs and convictions that will go a long way towards determining the kind of person I am and the way I live. Suppose we were to ask two different people a question: What is life all about? The first answers, "Life is about getting ahead. It means looking out for number one and getting the better of the other guy before he gets you. It means making a profit, feathering your own nest and doing whatever it takes to do so." The second person answers, "Life is about making a contribution to the world and to your fellow human beings. It's about making the world a better place and making whatever personal sacrifice is necessary to do so."

Here are two people with opposing views on the meaning of life. It is a safe bet that they are two different types of people, and we will probably like one more than the other. Yet they have something in common: neither can *prove* in any scientific or mathematical way that their way is the best way to live. The first cannot prove that looking out for ourselves should be the number one priority, though he or she may have arguments to support this view. The second cannot prove that generosity and self-sacrifice are the best approach to life, though he or she, too, may have arguments to support this view.

Our deepest beliefs and convictions are assumptions we make about life and the world. There is a difference between belief and knowledge. That water freezes at 0 degrees Celsius is knowledge that can be demonstrated scientifically. My knowledge of this fact is not my personal property; I share it with everyone else. Beliefs are different. Even though I share certain beliefs with others (as I do when I recite the Creed at Mass), in some sense those beliefs are uniquely mine, because they have a personal meaning for me. When we recite the Creed together at Mass and profess our belief that Jesus Christ was "born" or "incarnate" of the Virgin Mary," we are proclaiming a basic truth that we all share. And yet Mary can have a different and very personal meaning for various members of the assembly. My beliefs about what life ultimately means, about what is important and about how life is to be lived have much to do with making me the somebody I am. They give me a sense of who I am because they influence the way I think and feel and live my life.

I started this chapter with the statement "I believe, therefore I am a somebody." That is because my beliefs go a long way toward determining my character, my outlook on life, my values, what I think is important. Imagine a medical researcher who spends his life working towards a cure for a particular form of cancer. His knowledge of medical science makes it possible for him to carry out his research.

But it is his belief about what is important in life and how to live his life that motivates him to work for the benefit of humanity. His knowledge qualifies him as a scientist, but his beliefs and convictions make him the person he is. Some people will argue that beliefs are not important; it is how we live that counts. This is true in a "bottom line" sort of way, but it would be foolish to say that what we believe has nothing to do with the way we live. (Think of the two imaginary people, described above, who answered the question about the meaning of life.)

But what does all this have to do with the Creed? If the Creed is merely a prayer that I recite rather absent-mindedly and mechanically, then perhaps it has little to do with my sense of who I am. The Creed is a set of beliefs, but those beliefs will never contribute to my sense of being a somebody unless I make them my own deeply felt convictions. I can derive a sense of being somebody only from what is truly my own. This means that when I recite the Creed, it must be more than a set of dry, abstract statements about God, creation, the Trinity, the Incarnation, and so on. These statements must come from within me and say something about me.

Let's take a quick, preliminary trip through the Creed and, as we go, translate the various statements into what they say about me or anyone who recites the Creed with conviction.

I believe in God, the Father Almighty, creator of heaven and earth

I believe that I am not just the product of millions of years of blind evolution, but that ultimately am an expression of God's creative power and love. I believe that, as the Bible says, I am created in God's image and likeness and, therefore, have a special connection with God. The words "Father Almighty" remind me that, although he is the Almighty "Creator of heaven and earth," God nevertheless wants that connection to be a father-child relationship. I am not only God's creature but God's child.

And in Jesus Christ, his only Son, our Lord, who was conceived by the Holy Spirit, born of the Virgin Mary

I believe that Jesus Christ came to redeem me and everyone else from the wound in our human nature (sin) that mars the image of God in me. The words "born of the Virgin Mary" tell me that Jesus, though divine, was truly human because he was born of a human mother. If Jesus is the Son of God and I also am a child of God, then Jesus is like an older brother to me and Mary is also my mother. I have a heavenly Mother as well as a heavenly Father. I believe that Christ became a human being so he could express God's love for me in a human way – that is, in a way I can understand and appreciate. I believe that he demonstrated this by the way he spoke to the people, healed the sick, reached out to people whom everyone else had rejected, and hugged the children who wanted to talk to him when even some of his followers thought they were a nuisance.

Suffered under Pontius Pilate, was crucified, died and was buried; he descended into hell; on the third day he rose again from the dead

Dying for someone is the ultimate expression of love. I believe that Christ's death was the ultimate expression of God's love for me and that God became human in order to die a human death and express God's love in that way. I also believe that by rising from the dead, God has shown me that my own death is not the end – that my final destiny is not death but eternal life.

I believe in the Holy Spirit

I believe that God, in giving me the Holy Spirit, has given me a share in the Spirit of love that exists between God the Father and the Son – that is, a share in the Son's relationship with the Father. This, in turn, means that God the Father becomes my Father and I become God's child. I also believe that God has given me a special task: to bring God's Spirit into a world that is in need of it. It is my job to represent God's Spirit of love, understanding and compassion in the midst of the world's hatred and violence; the Spirit of justice in the midst of the world's injustice; the Spirit of simplicity and generosity in the midst of the world's greed; the Spirit of reverence and care for God's creation in the natural environment in the face of humanity's pollution and destruction of earth, air and water.

The holy catholic Church, the communion of saints

When I say that the Church is "holy," I don't mean that all its members are holy. I mean it is a holy gathering of people because God is present among them. Jesus said that where even two or three are gathered, he would be there among them. As a member of the Church I am part of something greater than myself – the worldwide community of all those who believe in Christ. When I go to Mass, I am not standing alone before God. There are other quiet times when I can do that and talk to God one-on-one. At Mass, I am taking a stand with other Catholics: when we recite the Creed together, we proclaim that we are people who believe in God's love for us and are trying to love God in return. Standing among the others at Mass reminds me that I am just as much a part of the community as anyone else, just as much the object of God's love as anyone else and, therefore, just as important in the eyes of God as anyone else. (When I am on my own, I may lose sight of all that.) And when I receive communion, I am sharing that communion with Catholics all over the world. There is a special feeling that goes with being part of a worldwide community. It gives me a sense of belonging that no one can take away from me. The "communion of saints" reminds me that this community is more than worldwide. It includes the saints in heaven and the souls in purgatory.

The forgiveness of sins

I believe in the forgiveness of sins because I believe that God is a loving Father, and loving fathers forgive their children when they make mistakes, even while encouraging them to do better. I believe that asking God for forgiveness helps to make me a more understanding and forgiving person.

The resurrection of the body, and life everlasting

I believe that the life God gave me when he made me his child and gave me his Holy Spirit is an eternal life that does not end with death. The words "resurrection of the body" are difficult to understand, but they tell me that God's love for me is not just love for my soul but for all of me – body and soul. If my body is a temple of the Holy Spirit, then my body holds the love of God within it.

The word "special" is often overused. When, however, I say that the Creed should make us feel "special," I am speaking of the sense of self, the feelings of dignity and self-esteem – the feeling of being a somebody – that we experience when we do good work or create something uniquely our own. The Creed gives us a spiritual and eternal foundation for that feeling of being a somebody.

Of course it would not do to recite the Creed in this way every time we say it. It is a prayer, after all, and prayer is not supposed to be a self-conscious effort to bolster our self-esteem. Prayer is meant to raise our minds and hearts to God. Still, it is good to remind ourselves from time to time of what the statements in the Creed mean to us personally and what they say about our dignity and worth as creatures and children of God, temples of the Holy Spirit, and members of the Church. If I think about this personal meaning of the Creed, I can say it with more personal devotion and conviction. It will become my personal creed, a set of beliefs that expresses who I am – my claim to be a somebody – and not just a formula to mumble without thinking because it is that time at Mass.

Saintly somebodies

Ignatius of Antioch died as a martyr in the year 107 in Rome, during the persecution of Christians carried out by the Roman emperor Trajan. Ignatius, who had been the bishop of Antioch, a city in the Roman province of Syria, was taken from there to Rome under armed guard to be put to death. On the journey he wrote a number of letters to various Christian communities. In a letter to the Christians of Rome, he begs them not to discourage him from going willingly to his death. Then he says something interesting. He asks the Romans to pray for his Church in Syria – the Church he had to leave behind. Even though he was the bishop of that Church, he confesses that he feels unworthy "even to be regarded as one of her members, for I am … the least of them." But then he adds, "But if I come to God, then, by his mercy, *I shall be someone*" (Ignatius to the Romans, 9; italics mine). Ignatius obviously thought that God's mercy, not his own achievements, made him a somebody. When we say the Creed, we, too, ultimately base our claim to be a somebody on what God has done for us in creating us, redeeming us, making us his children and members of God's Church. Our own achievements are important, of course, in giving us a sense of who we are; but for Christians, the good things we do are simply our way of acting in accordance with what the Creed tells us we are.

Another example of a "saintly somebody" is Joan of Arc. Joan was a French peasant girl living in the early 15th century, during the Hundred Years War, when English troops occupied much of France. At age 14, Joan began hearing voices, which she identified as those of saints Michael, Catherine of Alexandria and Margaret of Antioch. The voices urged her to "save France" by expelling the English. After donning white armour and leading the French troops in a series of successes, she was betrayed by her enemies and handed over to the English. They, along with those among the French who were their allies, condemned her as a heretic and had her burned at the stake at the age of 19.

Many people consider Joan a "martyr of conscience" because she refused to deny the truth of those voices that told her who she was and what she was meant to do. We can assume that Joan was a typical teenager who had to listen to other voices trying to answer those same questions for her: the voices of parents and friends, who must have been stunned by what she was doing; the voices of the officials at the king's court, who refused to take her seriously; and the voices of her accusers and judges at her trial, who told her she was a heretic and a witch. Though Joan's situation was much more dramatic than most, her task was that of every young person: to decide which of all the voices speaking to her she should listen to and take seriously.

Young people today have the same problem. They hear all kinds of voices telling them who they are, what they should do, how they should live, what is important and what is not. These voices – the voices of parents, friends, teachers, music, TV, movies, advertising, and so on – can be confusing to the young, who are not all that certain about their own identity. The process of becoming a somebody is not yet complete.

For all of us, the Creed is a voice that is well worth listening to. Of all the voices vying for our attention, the Creed tells us, at the most fundamental level, who we are and how we should live, what we should do and what is important. The Creed gives us as believers an identity. It makes us a somebody. Against all the voices that tell us to settle for less, the Creed tells us what we really are – children of a loving, forgiving God, the objects of an infinite and eternal love, and bearers of the Spirit of that love. St. Paul sums up everything the Creed says about us in these words: "We are God's work of art, created in Jesus Christ to live the good life as from the beginning he had meant us to live it" (Ephesians 2:10). A work of art is something to be cherished.

Baseball great Babe Ruth once said that he liked being a Catholic because "like a batting average, it sets a standard by which I can measure myself."[2] If we take the voice of the Creed seriously, it will give us a standard by which we can judge all the other voices that are trying to push us in one direction or another. To use that overused word again, everyone wants to be "special." If we let the Creed really speak to us, nothing will make us feel more special. No wonder so many have died as martyrs rather than deny the truth of what the Creed says to them and about them.

---

[2] Quoted in Michael Leach and Therese J. Borchard, eds. *I Like Being Catholic* (New York: Doubleday, 2000), 62.

Food for Thought

On belief vs. unbelief

Anyone who makes up his mind to evade the uncertainty of belief will have to experience the uncertainty of unbelief, which can never finally eliminate for certain the possibility that belief after all may be the truth. It is not until faith is rejected that its unrejectability becomes evident.

—Joseph Ratzinger (now Pope Benedict XVI), *Introduction to Christianity* (San Francisco: Ignatius Press, 2004), 45.

On conformity vs. individuality

As humans we are caught between competing drives, the drive to belong, to fit in and be part of something bigger than ourselves and the drive to let our deepest selves rise up, to walk alone, to refuse the accepted and the comfortable, and this can mean, at least for a time, acceptance of anguish. It is in the group that we discover what we have in common. It is as individuals that we discover a personal relationship with God.

—Jean Vanier. *Becoming Human* (Toronto: Anansi, 1998), 18–19.

2

The One God

I believe in God

Believing that God is

When we recite the Apostles' Creed, we begin with the words "I believe in God." This is a bold statement of belief because it amounts to a claim that our life has a divine and eternal source and goal. It is important, therefore, to understand what we are saying and why. The first thing to notice about this statement is that it begins with "I" – the first person singular. The only other prayer of the Mass that begins with "I" is "I confess" (the *Confiteor*), which takes place at the beginning of Mass as part of the Penitential Act. At that time we acknowledge that we have sinned and ask God for forgiveness.

These two statements – "I confess" and "I believe" – should tell us that we must take personal responsibility for two things – our sins and our faith. We cannot blame our moral failings on anyone else. In reciting the *Confiteor*, we take personal responsibility for the ways we have failed to live as a child of God. Taking responsibility is a sign of maturity. By the same token, we cannot duck responsibility for our own faith by saying, "Whatever the Church teaches is fine by me." We must try to understand the Creed and make it an expression of our personal beliefs. Or, as I suggested in Chapter 1, it must be an expression of who we are. If we have not made the Creed our own in this way, then it becomes rather meaningless to join with the others at Mass and say, "I believe." The recent change in the English translation of the Nicene Creed, from "We believe" to "I believe," emphasizes this aspect of personal responsibility.

The second thing we should notice about the statement "I believe in God" is that it comes right at the beginning of the Creed. We begin by stating our belief that God exists, that God is real. This truth is fundamental since without it, the rest of the Creed – which talks about the nature of God and what God has done for us – would not make sense. The Nicene Creed is a little more specific, stating, "I believe in *one* God." With these words we declare ourselves to be monotheists, people who believe in one God rather than many gods.

Monotheism is a belief that Christians have inherited from Judaism, because it was to the Jews that God revealed himself as the one true God. It became the mission of the Jews to preserve this belief in one God rather than many gods and to be witnesses to this belief to the pagan nations among whom they lived. The Jews were constantly reminded of their commitment to monotheism in their sacred writings: "Hear, O Israel, the Lord our God is one Lord" (Deuteronomy 6:4). Because we Christians derive our belief in one God from Judaism, we refer to the Jews – as Pope John Paul II did – as our "elder brothers in the faith," and in the Good Friday liturgy we pray for the Jews, "to whom the Lord our God spoke first."

When God revealed himself to Moses and, through Moses, to the whole Hebrew nation, he gave them what we call the Ten Commandments. The first commandment reminds the people that the Lord is their God, and adds, "You shall have no other gods before me" (Exodus 20:3). With these words God forbade the Jews to practise idolatry, the worshipping of any god other than the true God. This rule might seem obvious to us, since we believe in one God in the sense of being the only God who exists. It seems, however, that – at least in the beginning – the Jews were not really monotheists in this full sense. They did not necessarily deny the existence of other gods. They simply believed that their God (the Lord) was supreme over other gods and was the God who saved them by his power. (Psalm 94 proclaims, "The Lord is a great God and a great king above all gods.") They owed him their worship and allegiance.

It made sense for God to warn the Jews against worshipping those other gods. But the warning also has meaning for modern Christians. We are not likely to worship the sun or the moon or a pagan god, but we can commit idolatry by putting something else in the place of God, making it the most important thing in our lives, living only for it so that God gets lost in the shuffle. In such a case, we worship something and it takes the place of God in our lives. That something might be power or ambition or fame or pleasure or wealth. If one of these is all we live for, it has become a god of sorts because it claims our complete devotion. It will also affect the way we live, just as believing in the true God affects the way we live. We will probably treat people badly to get what we want and live for. Alcohol, drugs, overeating or gambling can become serious addictions. Any one of them can become "god" if it is what we live for. If God is the highest value in our lives, though, then every other value is relative, deriving its value from how it relates to that supreme value. In this way, a hierarchy of values is established that gives a certain unity to our personality and our life.

What I have said so far amounts to this: we must take personal responsibility for our belief in God, and our personal belief in God implies that we are making God the most important thing in our lives. God becomes a point of reference for everything in my life. All the rest becomes relative to this relationship with God, and the worth and importance of all is judged accordingly. Having God as a point of reference for our lives means we need not turn away from everyday life to find God. In the light of faith, everything in life points to God or refers us to God. In this way God is present in all the things that go on in our lives.

In saying we believe in God, we are actually making two statements. First, we believe that God exists. (This is usually what people mean.) Second, we have faith in the

God who has revealed not only his existence but also his love for us through the self-sacrificing love of Christ. This means we *trust* God when he talks to us about himself and about us and makes promises to us. When I say, "I believe in God," then, I am saying that I believe a truth and I believe a person: I have both believing faith and trusting faith. This is true of any statement we believe "on faith."

Imagine a history teacher who is teaching students about World War II and telling them that it lasted from 1939 to 1945. They dutifully make a note of that fact, reproduce it on a test and everyone is happy. The students have also made an act of faith. It is the same kind of double-barrelled faith as "I believe in God." They believed a truth about World War II, but they also believed their teacher. They believed in the teacher in the sense that they trusted him or her to give them accurate information. If the teacher were wrong about the dates, the students might be mildly annoyed, but not terribly upset. This piece of factual information can easily be corrected.

Now let's imagine another scenario. Imagine two lovers saying to each other, "I love you." This statement is not an objective piece of information like the dates of World War II. You are not likely to simply write it down and post it on the refrigerator door – next to the grocery list – so as not to forget it. This piece of information requires a much more personal response. If you believe this statement, your belief contains a much greater element of trust. Believing it and loving the other in return is an act of trust in that person. Your beloved is communicating his or her deepest feelings towards you – not just factual information, but subjective emotions. In this act of faith, trust plays a fundamental role. Because of its more personal nature, a lot more is at stake. Again we can see the difference between believing a truth and believing in – having a trusting faith in – a person. Now let's examine how that distinction applies to our belief in God. What is the difference between believing truths about God and believing in God?

Believing truths about God

In Chapter 1, I suggested that people generally live according to a set of beliefs. These beliefs are not necessarily ideas that can be scientifically or mathematically proven to be true. They are more in the nature of assumptions that people make about how things are and how things should be, about what life is about and how it should be lived. If a friend tells you that she believes people are basically good rather than evil, she may not be able to prove it. Instead, she might say she "knows it in her bones" or this is her "gut feeling." That gut feeling may not be provable, but it is the outcome of your friend's character, temperament and experience of life and other people. Here is the next question: Is this how we believe in God? Is it a "gut feeling" that we can't prove? Is it more intuitive than rational? Is it just how we feel because of who we are and the way life has treated us?

We have come to the question of why we believe a truth about God – that is, the truth of his existence. Since in this chapter we are dealing with the statement "I believe in God," our immediate question is "Why do I believe in God?" What grounds do I have for this belief? The moment we express a belief in God's existence, we place ourselves on the opposite side of the debate from those who deny the existence of God. The debate about the existence of God never seems to be settled by arguments. People may be atheists for any number of reasons; if they become believers, it is usually because of some life experience. They do not become believers by losing an argument about the existence of God. A believer's responsibility, then, is to be aware of the reasons behind his or her own belief, not to "convert" others with those reasons. Conversion is the work of God's grace. The best thing we can do for a nonbeliever is to explain why our belief makes sense *to us*. As St. Peter tells us, we should "always be prepared to make a defense to anyone who calls you to account for the hope that is in you." But then he adds, "Yet do it with gentleness and reverence" (1 Peter 3:15).

For some people, the question of the existence of God is a matter of indifference; for others, it is an exercise in philosophical argument in which God can become more an object of debate than an object of faith. To believers, however, the existence of God is a question that means something in everyday life. They care deeply whether God exists because God's existence tells them where they came from and what their ultimate goal is. My grade-school catechism began with the question "Why did God make me?" The answer was "God made me to know, love and serve him in this world and to be happy with him in the next." Little did I realize as a child that figuring out how best to do all that would be a lifelong task, but the answer is still correct, and it gives meaning and purpose to my life. The statement "God exists" means there is more to life than me and there is more to life than this world. Does it matter that God exists? To a believer, nothing matters more. The question of God is an existential question. It has more than intellectual or philosophical meaning. It means something for my very existence.

Christian tradition holds that the reason for our belief in God's existence is the fact that God has made his existence known to us. God has done this in two ways: by making himself known to us directly through the Old Testament prophets and in the person of Jesus Christ, and indirectly through creation. When I say indirectly, I mean that God lets us discover God's existence for ourselves by studying his handiwork in creation. By the very fact of creation – the fact that the universe exists – it is argued that there must be an intelligent being who created the universe. Let's take a simple example of something in the world that points to God as its source.

Imagine that two friends are arguing about which of two pieces of music is more beautiful. They argue back and forth until they agree to disagree. Even so, they agree on one point: there is such a thing as beauty. Otherwise the argument would make no sense. If there is no such thing as beauty, it would be silly to argue whether one piece of music is more beautiful than another. The world is full of beautiful people and things. And this refers to more than physical beauty. There is also artistic beauty (music, art, literature) and the spiritual beauty we find in the lives of people such as Mother Teresa. All these beautiful people or things are examples or expressions of what we can call beauty itself. And that is what we call God. God is not just someone beautiful but beauty itself, the absolute standard of beauty against which everything beautiful must be measured. If I say that Mozart's music is beautiful, I have in my mind some absolute standard of beauty upon which I am basing my judgment but which I cannot express or put into words. That absolute, inexpressible standard is what believers call God. It is inexpressible because although we know there is such a thing as beauty itself, we cannot describe or define it. We can only recognize it in beautiful things or people. It is the same with God. We cannot define or describe what God is any more than we can define what beauty is. We can, however, formulate arguments to support belief in God's existence because of the existence of people and things that reflect something of what God is, just as we know that beauty exists because beautiful things and people exist. That is why St. Thomas Aquinas said we can know *that* God is but we cannot know *what* he is.

To illustrate this concept, let's stay with the idea of beauty for a moment. Sometimes when I see a beautiful sunset, I believe I am getting a tiny glimpse of God the creator. You could say that the simple act of looking at the sunset has become a religious experience. Now that experience can become religious in one of two ways. First, I can think about the experience and construct an argument for the existence of God. The argument might go like this: There is no practical reason for a sunset – or anything else in nature – to be that beautiful. This kind of beauty is not strictly necessary. The universe would survive and continue to function if sunsets and sunrises and flowers and trees and mountains and lakes were ugly rather than beautiful. And the same goes for humanly created beauty. Humanity would survive and life would go on if Michelangelo or Shakespeare or Mozart had never been born. If none of the great art or music or literature ever existed, life would not be as rich or rewarding or as much fun, but we would survive. So why all this beauty if it is not strictly necessary? Could it be that somebody wanted to delight me? And that this somebody can only be a God who cares for his creatures? Could it be that a loving creator didn't just want me merely to survive, but wanted me to have a life worth living? Could it be that God our Father wanted to make the earth a beautiful home for us to live in? Could it be that God wanted us to be surrounded by beauty and not ugliness? Is that not what a good father wants for his children? This kind of argument is more suggestive than compelling, but it is an argument in support of what one already believes on faith.

There is another way in which I can encounter God in that beautiful sunset. Instead of thinking about it and constructing an argument, I can simply recognize that in this experience of beauty, I am experiencing God who is beauty itself. No thinking, no argument. I simply know immediately that I am somehow in the presence of God.

Even people who do not believe in God have experiences of this kind, which they might call transcendent experiences. They do not name what they are experiencing "God," but they feel themselves caught up in something greater than themselves, something that is above and beyond – that transcends – their ordinary, everyday human experience. It is as if the immediate experience is an expression of something deeper and more ultimate. Most people have had such experiences when encountering something incredibly beautiful or awe-inspiring. These are experiences that cannot be manufactured. They just happen. It is impossible to describe our feelings and reactions, although artists try to do so for us. If what we are ultimately experiencing is something of God, it is not surprising that we cannot express it, because God is beyond our control (transcendent) and beyond our power to describe (inexpressible or ineffable).

Many people who believe in God do so because they find the idea of God the only logical explanation for what they see around them. What I have been saying about beauty could also be said about things like truth and goodness. If our two argumentative friends are arguing about whether a kilometre is two thirds or three fifths of a mile, they are arguing about which statement is *true*, so they both obviously agree that there is such a thing as truth. Otherwise, why argue that one idea or fact is more true than another? Or, if they are arguing about which is better – ice cream or chocolate – they clearly agree that there is such a thing as goodness. There must be some absolute standard, not only of beauty but also of goodness and truth – something we can only call beauty itself, goodness itself and truth itself. There must be some ultimate source for the examples of beauty, goodness and truth we find in the world. What is that ultimate standard to be called?

Believers call it God. It's unfortunate that some people can only think of God as some kind of heavenly policeman who enforces rules. God is a loving God who shares something of himself with us in everything we experience that is true, good or beautiful. The Bible urges us to "taste and see that the Lord is good" (Psalm 34:8). Every time we experience something good (good food, good people, good times, and so on), we "taste" something of God, who is goodness itself. In the same way, with every truth we learn, we learn something about God who is truth itself. And in everything beautiful that we encounter, we experience something of God who is beauty itself. We think of God as "up there" and apart from us, but God has left glimpses and reminders of himself everywhere. If God were accused of creating the world, he would have to plead guilty. His fingerprints are all over it.

Believing in God

Let's recall the difference between a statement such as the dates of World War II and the statement "I love you." It should be obvious that the second statement requires much more trust on the part of the believer. Why? Because the statement and our belief in it have a much more personal meaning than a dry historical fact does, and, therefore, believing it expresses a great deal of trust in the other.

The response to "I love you" is not just one of intellectual belief, as it would be with historical dates or other factual information. Rather, it is the response of our whole person to another person. When someone says, "I love you," and you believe it and love the other person in return, you are not just storing information in your brain. You are creating a loving relationship.

Our faith in God is this kind of response. In the life, death and resurrection of Christ, God tells us something. God makes a statement. That statement is summarized in the Creed. When we recite the Creed, we express our faith in that statement. Reduced to its simplest terms, that statement is "I love you; I want you to be my children; I want you to live forever in my presence." Our response of faith is both a trusting belief in that statement and an effort to love God in return and live as his children. Faith, then, is more than believing the truth of certain doctrines about God. It is a response of one person to another person's love and promise – God's.

When we respond positively to another person's "I love you," our response has three parts. First, we believe the truth of the statement. Second, we have a trusting faith in the person who makes the statement. Third, we make a commitment to love the other person in return. When we recite the Creed with faith, our faith is supposed to have those same three qualities: we believe the truth of the statements in the Creed, trust the God who revealed these truths, and commit ourselves to live by what the Creed says we are – God's creatures, children and objects of his redeeming love. This is the only kind of faith that has an impact on our lives. If our faith is merely a matter of the mind – belief in the truth of certain doctrines – then it is like hearing someone say "I love you" and treating this statement like an impersonal piece of information. It is the same as believing last night's hockey scores.

I have been saying that, as Christians, our faith is a response to what God has said to us in the person of Christ. But God did not wait until the coming of Christ to teach us the meaning of faith. Long before Christ, God had taught people what faith was all about. Sometime between the years 2000 and 1500 BC, God called the patriarch Abraham to a life of this kind of faith. When the story (Genesis 12–25) opens, Abraham (then called Abram) is 75 years old and his wife Sarah (called Sarai) is 65. Clearly they are in their golden years and are not looking for any surprises. They have no children and obviously do not expect to have any. God, however, does surprise Abraham. He speaks to Abraham and tells him, along with Sarah, to leave his relatives and homeland and go to a foreign land. God does not even specify the country but simply tells Abraham to go to "the land I will show you." In return he promises Abraham something that, from a human point of view, is impossible. He promises that Sarah will give birth to a child; through that child, Abraham will become the father of a great nation. Moreover, the promised child does not arrive until Abraham is 100 and Sarah is 90! A biblical scholar might warn us not to take these numbers at face value. It is clear, however, that in this case, the numbers are intended to emphasize the faith of Abraham, who puts his faith in a promise that contradicts human reason and all human expectation.

Abraham's response to God's call is to act. The Bible simply states, "So Abraham went as the Lord had told him" (Genesis 12:4). But consider for a moment, the faith behind Abraham's obedience. First, he believed in God; he believed that the God who spoke to him was real. Second, his faith was an act of trusting belief in God. Think about how much trust it took for Abraham to leave his family and homeland behind, to give up all his sources of security (property, family, etc.), set off on this "crazy" adventure to which God was calling him, and put his faith in what seemed to be a ridiculous promise. Abraham's faith involves both believing a truth and trusting a person. It also contains that all-important third element: commitment to love God in return, carry out God's wishes, and live as God wanted him to live.

Eventually, God's promises to Abraham come true. Sarah gives birth to a son, Isaac. Through Isaac and his son Jacob, Abraham becomes the father of a great nation – the Jewish people. Christians understand the descendants of Abraham in a different way. Christian tradition identifies the spiritual children of Abraham as all those who have the same kind of faith Abraham had. When Christians put their faith in Christ and in God who is revealed in Christ, they, too, are responding to a call as Abraham did. God calls them to life in Christ – to faith in Christ and in God's love, which Christ reveals, to a sharing in Christ's relationship with the Father, and to a way of life in imitation of Christ. At the same time, God makes a promise: that our life will not end with physical death, but rather eternal life with God. This promise is – from a human point of view – just as impossible as the one he made to Abraham.

The Christian response to God's call requires the same kind of faith Abraham had: *belief* in the reality of the God who calls us; *trusting faith* in God's declaration of love and God's promises; and *commitment* to respond to that love and live as children of God. Because Abraham is a model of faith, Christians call him the "father of believers." At Mass we ask God to accept our offering "as you once were pleased to accept … the sacrifice of Abraham, our father in faith."

"I believe in God." We began this chapter by thinking about the importance of the first word in this declaration of belief – "I." Then we thought about God and God's existence. Finally we thought about faith, because faith connects the words "I" and "God." Faith is what connects us to God throughout our lives. We can throw it away or lose it, but no one can take it away from us. The martyrs who died for their faith prove that deeply held beliefs cannot be destroyed through violence.

Food for Thought

On finding God in creation

For what can be known about God is plain to them because God has shown it to them. Ever since the creation of the world his invisible nature, namely, his eternal power and deity, has been clearly perceived in the things that have been made.

—Letter of St. Paul to the Romans, 1:19-20

On finding God in beauty

Question the beauty of the earth, question the beauty of the sea, question the beauty of the air distending and diffusing itself, question the beauty of the sky … Question all these realities. All respond: "See, we are beautiful." Their beauty is a profession. These beauties are subject to change. Who made them if not the Beautiful One who is not subject to change?

—St. Augustine, Sermon 241, PL 38, 1134

3

The Trinity

I believe in God, the Father ...
and in Jesus Christ, his only Son ...
I believe in the Holy Spirit

What does "Trinity" mean?

When we say we believe in God, we are making an act of faith. In Chapter 2, I talked about some grounds for believing in God's existence that are based on reason and human experience rather than faith. We could argue that the very existence of the universe demands the existence of a creator, or that the examples of truth, goodness and beauty that we find in the world point to the existence of some absolute standard of truth, goodness and beauty. In the end, however, our belief in God is based on the fact that God has revealed himself through the Old Testament patriarchs and prophets and finally through his Son, Jesus Christ. The arguments from reason support our belief. They tell us that it is not contrary to reason to believe in God. The doctrine of the Holy Trinity, however, is a good example of a truth that we could not discover for ourselves. It has to do with God's inner life and nature; for that we need God to reveal himself – to talk to us about himself. Isn't it the same with human beings? You may know by hearsay that another person exists, but you really don't know anything about that person unless you meet him or her. In your conversation, something of the other's personality is revealed. Everything we say in the Creed is something God has told us about himself and about our relationship with God.

If you examine the Creed, you will see that the truths we profess to believe are divided into three groups. First, we profess our belief in God the Father as "Creator of heaven and earth." Then we profess our belief in "Jesus Christ, his only Son, our Lord," and in everything that Christ accomplished for our redemption: that God the Son became a human being by being born of the Virgin Mary, that he suffered and died for us, that he rose from the dead and ascended into heaven, and that he "will come to judge the living and the dead." Finally, we profess our faith in the Holy Spirit, the third Person of the Trinity.

The work of the Holy Spirit is to complete Christ's work of redemption by sanctifying those who believe in him. To sanctify means to "make holy" and the Holy Spirit does this by helping us to follow Christ's example and to live as children of God. When we conclude the Creed by stating our belief in the Church, the forgiveness of sins, the resurrection of the body, and eternal life, we are expressing our belief in the Holy Spirit, because all of these things are the works of the Holy Spirit. They are the consequences of God's gift of that Spirit. The Creed, then, is a statement of belief in God the Father, the Creator; God the Son, the Redeemer; and God the Holy Spirit, the Sanctifier.

If we take this kind of bird's-eye view of the Creed, it is easy to see that the Creed can be summarized as a statement of faith in the Holy Trinity. And this is as it should be. The Creed, after all, is a statement of Christian belief, and the Christian understanding of God is that in the one God are three divine Persons. Jews and Muslims worship the same God as Christians do, but the idea of God as a Trinity of Persons is unique to Christians. We should not be surprised, then, that the Christian Creed is an expression of faith in the Trinity. This being the case, let's stop and think about the meaning of this great Christian mystery.

Notice that I used the word "mystery" in reference to the Trinity. People commonly use the word "mystery" to describe something puzzling or baffling – a puzzle or riddle to be solved. The Trinity is certainly a mystery in this sense, because it is something beyond our ability to understand or explain logically. When I refer to myself and use the pronoun "I," clearly I am speaking of only one person – myself. According to the doctrine of the Trinity, when God says "I," God is referring to three Persons, and yet is talking about himself (singular) – the one God – just as I am talking about myself (singular). This idea is difficult for humans to grasp, because we cannot relate it to anything in our human experience.

Can the Trinity be understood?

Some Catholics seem to think that faith means nothing more than believing truths, such as that of the Trinity, that are beyond our human ability to understand. Could this be an easy way out, a way of rendering such truths meaningless so they have no impact on our lives and therefore make no demands on us? As mentioned in Chapter 2, faith involves much more than blind obedience. But surely if God has revealed himself as a Trinity of Persons, it was not just to confuse us and have us bow our heads and believe something we don't understand. It is safe to assume that whatever God reveals to us is for our benefit; therefore, it must be something that has meaning for us and for our lives. If the Trinity is part of God's revelation – part of what God wants us to know for our own benefit – then it must say something to us and about us. There must be a way of understanding the Trinity that tells us something both about God and about ourselves.

The Trinity might have more meaning for us if we think of the word "mystery" differently. For there is another sense in which the Church has used the word "mystery": the word can refer to a deeper truth that lies behind a more obvious truth or statement, a deeper spiritual reality behind some visible, tangible reality. A good example of this interpretation is found in the sacraments of the Church, which are sometimes referred to as "mysteries." When a person is baptized, the priest pours water over his or her head. To someone who does not believe in the sacrament of baptism, the priest simply seems to be washing the person's head. To a believing Christian, however, that simple act of cleansing is a *sign* that a deeper, spiritual cleansing is taking place. That deeper reality that is taking place is the cleansing of the baptized person from sin and rebirth to the life of grace. The pouring of the water in baptism is a *sacramental sign* of the forgiveness of sin and of the new life that the baptized person is beginning to live as a child of God.

Every sacrament is a visible sign of some invisible, spiritual reality or event. Let's look at the Trinity as such a mystery. The waters of baptism signify death and rebirth. The sign does not fully explain the spiritual death and rebirth that are taking place, but it helps us to gain some understanding by the use of an analogy. (An analogy is a comparison that gives us a human way of understanding something without fully explaining it.) So the sacramental sign can be seen as a human analogy to explain the spiritual effect of the sacrament. The sacramental signs – such as the water of baptism and the bread and wine of the Eucharist – are special because they are "effective" signs: they bring about the spiritual effect that they signify. Death and rebirth do take place in baptism; bread and wine do become the body and blood of Christ in the Eucharist.

Other analogies could help us to understand the effect of the sacrament. Here is an extremely homespun example. Have you noticed that taking a shower often makes you feel not only cleaner but better? It seems to give you a bit of a lift – a new lease on life, or at least on the day. After a shower someone might even say, "I feel like a new man/

new woman." That simple human experience can serve as an analogy to explain the fact that a newly baptized person is *cleansed and reborn* to a new life. The differences, of course, are enormous, but in both cases a new spirit and a new beginning are associated with cleansing. Can we find similar human analogies to help us understand the Trinity? The Trinity is a doctrine that describes the inner life and nature of God and, as already mentioned, is beyond the ability of our human minds to fully understand. But perhaps we can find something in our human experience that will serve as an analogy in helping us to find meaning in this doctrine.

The Apostles' Creed simply names the three Persons of the Trinity – Father, Son and Holy Spirit. The Nicene Creed, however, goes into a little more detail about the relationship among the three Persons. It says that the Son is "the Only Begotten Son of God," and that he is "begotten, not made, consubstantial with the Father." It says of the Holy Spirit that he "proceeds from the Father and the Son" and that "with the Father and the Son is adored and glorified." These words are intended to emphasize the fact that all three Persons are equally divine and equally eternal. The three Persons of the Trinity share one divine nature. What makes them distinct from one another is that the Son is "begotten" of the Father, while the Holy Spirit "proceeds" from the Father and the Son. Let's try a human make-believe analogy to try to understand this mystery.

Imagine that you are a citizen of Rome during the second century AD. As a devout follower of Roman religious customs, you are a card-carrying polytheist. You believe in the many gods that the Romans worship – Jupiter, Apollo, Diana, Venus and the rest. But you've heard about a new religion in town. Its members are called Christians and they are spreading the preposterous idea that there is only one God, who existed from all eternity and is the creator of heaven and earth. Your head is spinning with questions. If this god existed from all eternity, you ask, before anything was created, was the god not lonely? With whom did he associate? To whom did he speak? Before anything else existed, what did the god think about? These questions may seem silly to us, but they might have made sense to a second-century Roman who had never thought beyond the idea of many gods who associate with each other in a very human – sometimes all-too-human – way.

If our imaginary Roman were to take his questions to a Christian, he might have received this answer: The God that Christians worship is indeed the creator of all things. God is also above and apart from his creation and has no need of anything outside of himself. But this does not mean God is lonely or isolated or was unable to communicate with anyone even before anything was created. Why? Because in that one Christian God are three distinct Persons: Father, Son and Holy Spirit. That is why we say God is sovereign, that God is complete in himself and has no need of anything outside of himself. We humans need other people to live and make our way in the world, and even to become complete persons within ourselves. To become that "somebody" I talked about in Chapter 1, I need to relate to other people. I need community to become an individual. God does not have these needs. God is complete within himself because in himself he is a community of persons. (We shall come back to this idea later.)

Our inquisitive Roman, however, might still want to know how it comes about that there are three Persons in the one God. Or today we might ask: How is the Son "begotten" of the Father and how does the Holy Spirit "proceed" from the Father and the Son? Obviously to be "begotten" or to "proceed" does not mean to be born. That would make the Son and the Holy Spirit creatures of God. But the three Persons are all divine and eternal. To get some idea of the meaning of the word "begotten" in the Trinity, let's try another analogy.

Imagine a man looking at himself in a mirror. If that mirror is dirty and badly scratched, he will get a very imperfect image or reflection of himself. Or, if it is one of those oddly shaped mirrors in an amusement park house of mirrors, he might get a hilariously distorted image of himself. If, however, the mirror is perfectly flat, clean and polished, he will get a very good reflection of himself. The image in the mirror will look exactly like him. Now push this idea to a ridiculous extreme. Imagine that the image in the mirror is so perfect that it is another person who is the exact image of that man – another man who is an exact replica of the man looking into the mirror and, therefore, an expression of everything that the first man is.

Keeping in mind that we are talking about God in a human way, this example nevertheless gives us a way of imagining how the Son proceeds from the Father. Before God created the universe, we must imagine God existing by himself (because we can't comprehend the idea of eternity). If nothing else exists except God, what does God think about? The only possible answer is *himself.* We can imagine, then, God having within himself from all eternity an idea or thought or mental image of himself. Since this is God we are talking about, that thought or idea or image that God has of himself is perfect (unlike human self-understanding, which never seems to be perfect). And, just like that perfect mirror image in our example, it is so perfect that it is another person. We may think of God the Son, then, as – to speak in a human way – the Father's idea or image of himself that exists in the mind of God from all eternity. Because that idea or image is so perfect that it is a person, that person is the perfect image and expression of what the Father is. This Person is thus as eternal and divine as the Father.

When you and I want to express a thought or an idea, we use words. That is why we refer to God the Son – who is the perfect expression of the Father's divine nature – as the "Word of God." He is the Word because he is the perfect expression of a thought or idea – of God the Father's idea or image of himself. St. John begins his gospel in this way: "In the beginning was the Word: The Word was with God and the Word was God" (John 1:1). To put it another way, when we use words, we not only express our thoughts, we express ourselves. My way of expressing myself reveals something of the person I am. God's Word is the expression of who God is. These analogies do not explain the Trinity, but rather suggest a human way of imagining the Trinity. They approximate, in a human way, a reality beyond human understanding.

We can think about the Holy Spirit proceeding from the Father and Son in a similar way. If the Son is the Word of God, the Holy Spirit is the love of God. If the Son is the Father's idea or image of himself, which is such a perfect expression of the Father's nature that it is another Person, then we now have two Persons – Father and Son. And where there are two persons, a personal relationship exists between them. In the case of love between the Father and Son, that love is so perfect that it is another Person. The Holy Spirit, then, is the love that exists between the Father and the Son. The Holy Spirit personifies that love or, in theological language, is the substantial love of the Father and Son. That is why we say that when we receive the Holy Spirit, we become children of God – because we are given a share in the love that exists between the Father and the Son, and thereby share in the Son's relationship with the Father. To share in that relationship is to become a child of God. To receive the Holy Spirit is to receive the love of God. As St. Paul said, "God's love has been poured into our hearts through the Holy Spirit who has been given to us" (Romans 5:5).

Let's examine another human analogy. A man and a woman fall in love, get married and have a child. That child is the result of the love of his or her parents. We could say that the child is an expression of the love of the mother and father. The Holy Spirit as a person expresses the love between Father and Son just as a child, as a person – by his or her very existence – expresses the love of the mother and father. Obviously they are not the same thing, but the comparison lies in the fact that in both cases, a person is the expression of a loving relationship.

What does the Trinity say about us?

These simple analogies may help us to understand the Trinity. I have emphasized the fact that the Trinity explains why God is complete in himself and, unlike us, has no need of anything outside of himself: because he is a Trinity of Persons within himself. God has within himself that community of persons that you and I must go outside of ourselves to find. But does all this have any meaning for us and our lives? My answer is this: since, as children of God, we are all called to be like God, we need to understand what God is like. I believe that the doctrine of the Trinity tells us at least two important things about ourselves in our efforts to be like God.

(1) *To be like God is to do good unselfishly.* If God – because God is a Trinity of Persons – has no need of anything beyond himself, then God did not create us because he needed us. God created us purely and simply out of God's own goodness, because God wanted to share life with his creatures. Our best human analogy might be the case of someone who is such a good person that he or she seems to

be naturally kind and generous and understanding. It is as if that person just can't help being good. Goodness seems to be an expression of who the person is. Goodness is like that. It overflows. It can't remain within a good person; it must spread itself around. That is what God is like. God is – as I suggested in Chapter 2 – "goodness itself." And God's goodness, like the goodness of a good human being, has to express itself. Creation is the expression of God's goodness. If you want to be like God, you can't fake goodness simply by doing good deeds – dutifully or even grudgingly. Such deeds are still good, as far as they go, but they are not "God-like." To be God-like, good deeds must be an expression of inner goodness. For our actions to be good in a God-like way our minds, hearts and intentions must be good. Kind and loving deeds should come from a heart that truly loves others. God-like goodness is altruistic. Rather than doing good things for the sake of what's in it for us, or to satisfy some personal need, we do them for the sake of others. God's goodness in the act of creation does not express any need or self-interest on God's part and, ideally, our acts of goodness should be the same. Human beings, of course, are not capable of duplicating God's unselfishness, because we are not free of self-interest in the way God is. However, God's way remains the ideal, and the closer we come to that ideal, the more God-like we are.

(2) *Human beings cannot be God-like in the same way that God is.* Imagine those people who think of themselves as self-sufficient, self-made and having no need of anyone else. They are aloof, self-centred and contemptuous of

others. They push other people around and wield authority like a dictator. Such people are often described as "playing God." And yet it is impossible for a human being to be God-like in this way. Only God can be self-sufficient, complete in himself, and having no need of anything beyond himself. We need other people to become fully human. We cannot be like God in the way that God is in himself – as God is revealed to be in the doctrine of the Trinity. We must strive to be like God, but in a human way. How are we to do this? God gave us the answer to this question when God the Son became human – when "the Word became flesh" – in the person of Jesus Christ. As Pope Benedict has put it, in the person of Christ God becomes a God "with a human face." When this happened, it was as if God were saying, "This is what I would be like if I were a human being. If you want to be God-like in a human way, imitate my Son, Jesus Christ."

The pattern of Jesus' life is the exact opposite of the aloof, arrogant contempt for others displayed by those who "play God." Christ's life was one of care and concern for and service to others, to the point of giving up his life for them. That is how a human being becomes God-like. As Jesus himself said, "Whoever would be great among you must be your servant, and whoever would be first must be your slave, even as the Son of Man came not to be served but to serve and to give his life as a ransom for many" (Matthew 20:26-28). To be like God in a human way means to imitate the humanity of Christ.

Food for Thought

On the Trinity

By the grace of Baptism "in the name of the Father and of the Son and of the Holy Spirit," we are called to share in the life of the Blessed Trinity, here on earth in the obscurity of faith and after death in eternal light.

—*Catechism of the Catholic Church,* #265

On how the Trinity can be one God

God stands above singular and plural. He bursts both categories. ...... To him who believes in God as tri-une, the highest unity is not the unity of inflexible monotony. The model of unity or oneness toward which one should strive is consequently not the indivisibility of the atom, the smallest unity, which cannot be divided up any further; the authentic acme of unity is the unity created by love. The multi-unity that grows in love is a more radical, truer unity than the unity of the "atom."

—Joseph Ratzinger (now Pope Benedict XVI), *Introduction to Christianity* (San Francisco: Ignatius Press, 2004), 179.

4

Creator and Father

The Father almighty,
Creator of heaven and earth.

Did God create the world?

Two Catholics are sitting side by side at Sunday Mass. At the appropriate moment they stand together with the rest of the congregation and recite the Nicene Creed. Together they profess their belief in God the Father as "maker of heaven and earth, of all things visible and invisible." Both have expressed the belief that God is the creator of the world and everything in it. However, while one of these two Catholics fully accepts the theory of evolution, the other believes that God literally created the universe in six days, as described in the Book of Genesis. Are they both believing Catholics? If they both believe that God is the "creator of heaven and earth," then the answer is yes, for that is all the Creed asks them to believe. The Creed affirms that God is the creator of the universe. It does not specify how that creation was accomplished. (Genesis offers such an account, but in language that is clearly mythical: it contains truth, but is not historically true.) Current Church teaching is open to the theory of evolution as a hypothetical explanation for the creation of humanity, but insists that God is the creative power behind that process.

Some people seem to think that there is some kind of contradiction between these two ideas – the world as God's creation versus the world as developing through a process of evolution. The notion that these two ideas are incompatible seems to be based on a misunderstanding of either the theory of evolution or the doctrine of creation. Some fundamentalist Christians take the biblical account of creation in Genesis 1 literally. This means they must reject the theory of evolution because – taken literally – Genesis 1 describes the first humans as created directly by God rather than evolving from lower forms of life. On the other hand, the theory of evolution contradicts the idea of the world as God's creation only if we misunderstand what evolution is. This theory does not try to explain the origin of life. Charles Darwin, who first proposed the theory, did not try to explain the origin of life. His book *The Origin of Species* was an attempt to explain how the various forms or kinds or species of plant and animal life evolved from lower forms of life. Darwin himself believed that the question of how the evolutionary process all began – the question of the absolute beginning or origin of life – was a question that science could not answer.

So when we profess our belief in God as "creator of heaven and earth," we are not contradicting the theory of evolution properly understood. We are stating our belief in something that the theory of evolution cannot and does not try to explain. And when we express our acceptance of the theory of evolution, we are not contradicting the doctrine of creation unless, of course, we believe that everything – earth, air, water, fish, birds, animals, human beings – were all created directly over a six-day period. The concept of evolution certainly contradicts this version of creation, but it does not contradict the doctrine of creation as such, because it does not contradict the idea of God as the ultimate cause and origin of the whole process of evolution. The current debate between "creationists" and "evolutionists" is a debate between those who claim too much for the doctrine of creation (creation in six days) and those who claim too much for the theory of evolution (as explaining the very origin of life). It seems to be a false debate.

How should we treat God's creation?

The cause and effect argument for the existence of God – that is, the argument that there must be a First Cause that itself is uncaused to account for the beginning of the whole process of cause and effect, including the process of evolution – is also a good illustration of something fundamental in Catholic teaching and tradition about the attitude we should have towards the world God created. Thomas Aquinas found God when he looked at the world of nature, and Catholic tradition has always stressed this point. The world is a place where we can meet God. When we look at the natural world, we can come to the conviction that God exists and that he is the Creator – the First Cause – of everything. But, as I mentioned in Chapter 2, we can also discover God as the source of the goodness, truth and beauty that we find in the world. Some Christians seem to believe that human beings are so sinful, there is no way we can know anything about God in this way. They believe that God is so totally above and beyond us that we can know him only when he speaks to us directly. They therefore put all their emphasis on knowing God only through his revelation of himself in the words of the Bible. Catholics, of course, agree that we cannot know truths – such as the Trinity, or God the Son as our redeemer, or the Holy Spirit as sanctifier, or the promise of eternal life – unless God reveals them to us. But Catholic tradition also emphasizes that God is not unknowable apart from God's direct revelation: that he "speaks" to us in the beauty and goodness of his creation. We could say, then, that whenever we learn something new and interesting, we are getting a glimpse of truth itself, that is, God. Whenever we hear a great piece of music, we are getting a glimpse of beauty itself, that is, God. And whenever we read stories of selfless heroism or kindness, we are getting a glimpse of goodness itself, that is, God.

If it is true that we can find the beauty and goodness of God in his creation, then surely it is because the world, as God created, it is beautiful and good. The biblical account of creation ends with these words: "And God saw everything that he had made and, behold, it was very good" (Genesis 1:31). When it is said that the world and all material things in it are good "as God created them," it means they are good *in themselves*. It is good to remember that nothing in God's creation is evil in itself. Created things are God's gifts to us for our benefit and enjoyment. If there is evil, it is in the way we human beings misuse or abuse these gifts. Sex, drugs and alcohol are good examples. If used the way they were intended to be used, they contribute to our well-being and happiness. If misused, they can destroy not only individual lives but also careers, friendships, marriages and families.

St. Augustine said, "Whatever is, is good." And it is good because it is created by God, who is goodness itself. The created world reflects God's goodness. Moreover, God the Son made himself part of that material creation by taking on a human, physical body to carry out the work of our salvation. As the fourth gospel puts it, "The Word became flesh" (John 1:14). God, in other words, became a real flesh-and-blood human being. And the Church, in the sacraments, uses material elements of God's creation – water, oil, bread, wine – to celebrate the continuing presence among us of the Christ who imparts God's grace to us. These material things are "visible signs of grace," just as Christ's physical body was a visible sign of God's presence among us. So not only is the material world good because God created it; it is also *sanctified* (made holy) because of its role in our salvation.

The following prayer is said at mass on the twentieth Sunday in Ordinary Time:

O God, who have prepared for those who love you
good things which no eye can see,
fill our hearts, we pray, with the warmth of your love,
so that, loving you in all things and above all things,
we may attain your promises,
which surpass every human desire.

This prayer tells us three things about the attitude we should have towards God's creation and all the material things in it. First, God is to be found "in all things," that is, in the truth, beauty and goodness of his creation. Second, loving all the good things of creation is meant to lead us to love God as their creator. Created things have two purposes: they are God's gift meant for our enjoyment, but that very enjoyment is meant to lead us to love God "above all things," even more than his created gifts to us. (Is it not true, when we receive a gift, that we may love the gift but love the giver even more?) Third, the joy we find in the good things of creation is a joy that God will make complete in eternity. That joy of eternal life, we are told, will be joys "which surpass every human desire." It follows, then, that the joy we derive from the proper use of God's gifts in this life is a foretaste of those joys "which surpass every human desire." How can we desire the joy of heaven if we have no foretaste of it here and now – if we don't know what joy is?

In his book *The Catholic Experience,* Lawrence Cunningham writes, "The sacramental view of reality, like prayer, is an attitude prior to its being formalized as a sacramental act or series of acts."[3] The formalized sacramental

---

[3] Lawrence Cunningham, *The Catholic Experience* (New York: Crossroad, 1985), 115–16.

acts are, of course, the seven sacraments of the Church. The sacramental attitude that Cunningham speaks of is the habit of seeing, through the eyes of faith, the visible realities of the world as mediating – as communicating to us – the invisible reality of God's saving grace. Like the seven sacraments, they are "effective signs" of God's power and presence in the world. Watching a beautiful sunset becomes a religious experience of God precisely because I already believe in God and I am looking at the sunset with the eyes of faith. I have developed what Cunningham calls a "sacramental vision" towards the visible realities of the world, so I am "conditioned" to see the presence of God in the natural world. When I bring this faith-inspired sacramental vision to the natural world, that world "speaks back" to me in the sense that it strengthens the faith that I bring to the experience. This kind of sacramental vision is basic to Catholic spirituality; historically, this is why the Church has put such an emphasis on communicating the faith through art, music and ritual. To be Catholic means to appreciate that God is encountered not only in words and ideas but through the senses as well. This is why the prayer quoted above can speak of loving God "in all things," because in some real sense God is truly "in" the world of visible reality. This is a God one can not only love in an abstract, rational way, but, in some way, "fall in love with," as saints like Francis of Assisi did.

We can encounter God in the visible reality of the world as well by encountering, loving and serving God in other people. God, as we know, has revealed himself to us primarily in a person – the person of his son, Jesus Christ. That is why theologians sometimes refer to Christ as the "sacrament of God," since through the tangible, visible reality of his humanity, Christ reveals the invisible God. By taking on a human nature, Christ sanctified and raised to a higher level that human nature we all share with him. Because of this shared humanity with Christ, human beings become signs of the presence of Christ in the world, just as Christ was a sign of the presence of God. That is why we are encouraged to "see Christ" in others and to love and serve them as we would love and serve Christ. As Christ himself assured us, "Truly I say to you, as you did it to one of the least of these my brethren, you did it to me" (Matthew 25:40). Just as Christ suffered and was rejected, we are encouraged to see the presence of Christ in the suffering and rejected members of humanity: the hungry, the homeless, the stranger, the sick, the poor, the prisoner (see Matthew 25). We look at the natural world not just to construct rational arguments for the existence of God, but also to *experience the presence of God.*

Perhaps the attitude we should have towards God's creation could be summed up in these three simple rules.

(1) *Enjoy God's creation.* Created things are gifts from God. He is the ultimate creative force behind not only the created universe but also the books, movies, TV shows, CDs, concerts, plays, etc. that we enjoy. The list is endless. God wants us to use and enjoy all these things. In the prayer quoted above, we ask God to help us to love him *in and above* all these things, not *instead of* all these things.

(2) *Be grateful for God's creation*. It would be inconsiderate to enjoy a gift and not thank the one who gave it to you. It seems only natural, then, to thank God for all the good things God has created. Some people seem to think of prayer only as asking God for something, but surely God, like any gift giver, would like to hear an occasional and sincere "thank you." The Mass or Eucharist – that great prayer of thanksgiving – presents an opportunity to do this.

(3) *Take care of God's creation*. The first meaning of this rule is that we should not misuse or abuse any of the gifts of God's creation. Sex can be an expression of love or of selfishness. Drugs can save lives or ruin them. Alcohol can make life enjoyable or miserable. It all depends on how these things are used. Like all gifts they must be used as intended by the giver. At a higher level, the same applies to other human beings. Every injury to another human being, every lie told about another, every exploiting or cheating of another, every advantage taken of another – is an abuse not only of one of God's creatures, but of one of God's children.

Taking care of God's creation carries a further responsibility: we must look after the world God has given us. If you read the creation story in the Bible, you will see that once God has created the world and then the first humans, he puts them in charge of it. Adam and Eve represent all of us. We are the "masters" of creation. We are supposed to "subdue" it and have "dominion" over it and use what it produces for our own benefit. Subduing the earth, however, does not mean doing whatever we want with it. (Tilling the earth in order to make it productive and support human life is a good example of "subduing" the earth in a positive way.) The earth will not support us unless we take care of the fragile environment in which God has placed us. Polluted air, lakes and rivers all remind us of this responsibility. The world is not our property; it is like a house we have rented from God, who expects us to look after it. When we damage, exploit and pollute the natural environment, we are making a mess of the house we have rented from God.

Why do we call God "Father"?

Have you ever wondered why the line of the Creed we are discussing does not simply say "God the almighty, creator of heaven and earth" but "God the *Father* almighty, creator of heaven and earth"? The word "Father," of course, emphasizes the fact that God the Father – the first Person of the Trinity – is the creator. Creation is associated with God the Father, just as redemption is associated with the Son and sanctification with the Holy Spirit. But the word "Father" also emphasizes the fact that the one who created us also adopted us as his children and wants us to look upon him and relate to him as a father. He does not want us to think of him only in some cold abstract way as "First Cause" or "Supreme Being," but also as "Father." We know that God is a mystery beyond our understanding, so when we profess our belief in God as our Father, we are not defining what God is in himself; we are describing what God is *to us* and as he wants to be known to us – as Father who cares for all his children together and for each one individually.

Now, however, we are faced with another question. Does the image of God as Father adequately explain what God is for us? Does it really answer our religious needs or do we also need a mother – a goddess? Under ordinary circumstances, anyone who has been raised by both a mother and a father appreciates that diversity and would not want to lose either of them. And if having both a mother and a father is the ideal for our human lives, should it not also be the ideal for our spiritual lives? Some people find the image of God as Father to be too one-sidedly masculine or patriarchal. The Bible tells us that all of us – male and female – are created in God's image. If we think of God only in masculine terms – as Father – how do women and girls reflect the image of God? This has led to pointless debates about the "gender" of God and references to God as "she" rather than "he." This of course only creates an opposite kind of one-sidedness. God, of course, is neither male nor female. God is beyond gender.

But if God is neither male nor female, why do we think of God in terms of such a masculine image – as Father? The most obvious answer is that this is the image God used in revealing himself to us. He wanted us to think of him as Father and of ourselves as his children. In doing so, God adapted himself to our way of thinking. If we humans think of God as a person – which is the only way we can think about him or pray to him – then we must think of him as either masculine or feminine, because, to our human way of thinking, a person has to be masculine or feminine. When we describe God in this way, however, we are not describing what God really is. All we can say is that since God has encouraged us to think of him as Father, it tells us something true about God. Calling God "Father" might not seem so one-sidedly masculine if we understand that "father" does not simply mean "male." Here are a few points to remember when thinking about this question.

(1) The fact that God is revealed to us as Father does not mean God is exclusively "masculine" or that only males are made in the image of God. The biblical creation story states, "God created man in his image; in the divine image he created him;" and then it adds, "male and female he created them" (Genesis 1:27). What this passage seems to clearly say is that it takes both male and female – masculine and feminine – to represent or reflect the image of God. A man by himself is an incomplete image of God and a woman by herself is an incomplete image of God. Only *together* do they reflect God's image. This means that if we think of God in a human way – which is the only way we can think of God – then we must think of God as having both "masculine" and "feminine" qualities.

(2) This in turn means that if we humans are going to be images of God or reflect God's image, we must have both masculine and feminine qualities. The so-called masculine qualities are things like courage, steadfastness and devotion to duty. The so-called feminine qualities are things like tenderness, compassion and a nurturing instinct. I am using the qualifier "so-called" because it should be obvious that neither sex has a monopoly on either set of qualities. In order to be a complete human being, a person needs

to have both "masculine" and "feminine" qualities. Being a good father takes more than being a man and being a good mother takes more than being a woman. A good father must have "motherly" qualities and a good mother must have "fatherly" qualities. Single parents especially know how important this is. So if we think of God as a good father, it means that God also has motherly qualities.

(3) Think for a moment about the feminine or motherly qualities of God. Jesus Christ is the "Son" of God and certainly a masculine figure. There is no doubt about his "masculine" qualities of courage and steadfastness. At the same time, Christ is well known for the so-called feminine qualities of tenderness and compassion. We see this in his attitude to children, sinners and those who were rejected by the society in which he lived – foreigners, lepers, and others. There was nothing macho about Christ. He cried when his friend Lazarus died. He described his love for his own people in terms of motherly love: "How often would I have gathered your children together, as a hen gathers her brood under her wings" (Matthew 23:37). As the Son of God, Christ is the perfect image of God the Father, so the masculine and feminine qualities we see in him must also belong to God the Father. In the Old Testament, the prophet Isaiah described the love of God for his people in the same way: "You shall be carried upon her hip and dandled upon her knees. As one whom his mother comforts, so I will comfort you" (Isaiah 66:12-13).

(4) In the Catholic tradition, we can find certain images that remind us of the feminine side of God and help

us to avoid thinking of God in an exclusively masculine or patriarchal way. One of these images is the image of the Church as "mother." It used to be common for Catholics to refer to the Church as "Holy Mother Church." Obviously, such a title can be abused, keeping us in the state of obedient little children, even when we are grown up. On the other hand, when properly understood, it can be a way of emphasizing the Church's "motherly" role in our lives – in teaching us, nurturing us in the faith and protecting us. The Church as mother is an image that balances the image of God as Father. Another balance is provided by the image of the Virgin Mary. Mary, of course, is not divine; she is human. Nevertheless, in the role she plays in humanity's salvation, she in some way does for us what the goddesses of the ancient religions did for their worshippers. She reflects the "feminine" side of God. In Catholic teaching, after Jesus, no human being more perfectly reflects the image of God than Mary – *a woman*. People who criticize Catholic devotion to Mary seem to be unaware of this powerful effect she has on how Catholics think about God.

Food for Thought

Finding God in the laws of nature

The order and harmony of the created world results from the diversity of beings and from the relationships which exist among them. Man discovers them progressively as the laws of nature. They call forth the admiration of scholars. The beauty of creation reflects the infinite beauty of the Creator and ought to inspire the respect and submission of man's intellect and will.

— *Catechism of the Catholic Church,* #341

Something seems to compel physical objects to obey the laws of nature and what makes this observation odd is just that neither compulsion nor obedience are physical ideas.

Medieval theologians understood the question and they appreciated its power. They offered in response the answer that to their way of thinking made intuitive sense: *Deus est ubique conservans mundum.* God is everywhere conserving the world. It is *God* that makes the electron follow *His* laws.

— From David Berlinski, *The Devil's Delusion* (New York: Crown Forum, 2008), 132.

How do we come to an awareness of God?

In fact it is not all that common to meet someone who has come to a knowledge of God through the use of his or her reason alone; rarely do people argue themselves into belief or acceptance of God. If people come to a knowledge of God at all in that way, it is not usually through a strict dialectical [rational] process but through the much less schematic means of simply being awestruck by the beauty and complexity in the world around them.

— From Lawrence Cunningham, *The Catholic Experience* (New York: Crossroad, 1985), 124.

5

Son of God, Son of Mary

And in Jesus Christ, his only Son, our Lord,
who was conceived by the Holy Spirit,
born of the Virgin Mary

Jesus Christ

According to the Annunciation story, the angel Gabriel said to Mary, "Behold, you will conceive in your womb and bear a son and you shall call his name Jesus" (Luke 1:31). When, therefore, Joseph and Mary took the baby Jesus to have him circumcised eight days after his birth, St. Luke reports that "he was called Jesus, the name given by the angel before he was conceived in the womb" (Luke 2:21). Each one of us was also given a name when we were baptized. That name becomes a part of who we are, and so we develop a kind of attachment to it. It is something that is *ours* in a very personal way. Our name may also have a specific meaning, to which we generally don't give much thought.

At the time when Jesus was born, however, and among the Jewish people to whom he belonged, names were significant. A name was closely connected with the person who bore it and said more about him or her. To dishonour a person's name was to dishonour the person. That is why the commandment "You shall not take the name of the Lord your God in vain" meant something to the Jews. For them, to use God's name blasphemously or disrespectfully or carelessly was to dishonour God. Even today, devout Jews might avoid writing the word "God," substituting "G-d." This connection between the name and the person was particularly important in cases where God gave a person a particular name directly. In this case, the name often indicates the task or mission to which God is calling that person. And so it was with Jesus. The name tells us who he is and what he was meant to do. The angel told Mary to call him "Jesus" because this name – "Joshua" in Hebrew – means "God is salvation." When we use the name "Jesus," then, we profess our belief in the fact that he is our saviour – the one who accomplished our salvation.

But what about the other part of Jesus' name? Jesus is also called "Christ." We have become so used to saying "Jesus Christ" that it almost sounds as if "Christ" were Jesus' last name, and we could address him as "Mr. Christ." In fact, the word "Christ" is a descriptive word or title that tells us who Jesus was and what he means to us. Some famous people have such a word attached to their names to distinguish them from others with the same name. For example, there have been many Pope Gregorys but only one

"Gregory the Great." There are many St. Johns, but only one "John the Evangelist." The word "Christ" is a translation of the Greek *Christos* and the Latin *Christus*. These words in turn are a translation of the Hebrew word for "Messiah."

The word "Messiah" refers to the promised saviour the Jewish people hoped for and means "the anointed one." Among the Jews, two types of persons were anointed – kings and priests. Both kings and priests were seen as representatives of God who were called to carry out a special task in God's name. The anointing was a ceremony intended to call the Spirit of God upon the king or priest so he would be strengthened – oil is a symbol of strength – to carry out his task in God's name. Today, when a priest is ordained, he is anointed with oil for the same reason. Anointing with oil is also part of the ritual of both baptism and confirmation, because a Christian has a task to carry out in God's name and needs the Spirit of God's love to do so. In the sacrament of the anointing of the sick, oil again signifies a strengthening of the recipient in the face of suffering and death. Jesus is both a king and a priest: a king because he rules a kingdom (though a spiritual one) and a priest because he offered a sacrifice (of himself) for our salvation. He is therefore the anointed one – the Christ or the Messiah. Strictly speaking, it is more accurate to call him "Jesus *the* Christ" – "Jesus the anointed one." It is perfectly all right, however, to say "Jesus Christ," though it is important to remember what this term means. In some very Catholic countries, it is common for men to have the name Jesus. But there is only one Jesus the Christ.

Jesus Christ: God and man

When the angel told Mary that she was going to give birth to a child, she replied, "How can this be, since I have no husband?" (Luke 1:34). Mary was unmarried and a virgin. How could she possibly give birth to a child? The angel replied, "The Holy Spirit will come upon you and the power of the most high will overshadow you; therefore the child to be born will be called holy, the Son of God" (Luke 1:34-35). This little story tells us two things about Jesus: first, that Jesus was truly human because he was born of a human mother – a Jewish girl named Mary who lived in the town of Nazareth; and second, that Jesus was also truly divine, because his father was not a human father but God. As the angel said to Mary, she would not become pregnant through any human means, but through the action of the "Holy Spirit" and "the power of the Most High." We might think of it this way. A baby is the result of the love between a human father and mother, and therefore has the same human nature as they do. Jesus is the result of the love between a human mother and a divine father, and thus has both a human nature and a divine nature.

This means that Jesus is both God and man. He is both the Son of God and the son of Mary. God the Son – the second Person of the Trinity – who was fully divine became fully human by taking on a human nature from the Virgin Mary. As the Creed says, Jesus "was conceived by the Holy Spirit, born of the Virgin Mary." In Chapter 3, I referred to the second Person of the Trinity as the "Word." The Son is the perfect expression of the Father's divine nature, just as the word I speak expresses the thought in my mind. When we say that the Word "became flesh," we mean that God became human. This perfect expression of the Father became a human being, expressing what God is, but in a human way.

When the word "flesh" is used in the Bible, it often means not simply flesh as we understand it – our bodies – but rather our human nature. (Sometimes the word "flesh" is used in a negative way to mean our all-too-human nature, as when St. Paul writes about the conflict between "flesh" and "spirit.") That is why we call this doctrine about Christ the doctrine of the Incarnation. The Latin word *caro* means "flesh"; the Incarnation refers to God the Son becoming "enfleshed" or "incarnated," taking on our "flesh" or human nature. What makes this truth a "mystery" and difficult to understand is that while Christ has two natures – human and divine – he is *one person*.

In the early centuries of the Church's history, there was a great deal of argument and controversy about the nature of Christ, or at least over how to express it doctrinally. Was Christ human or divine? Some claimed that Christ was a divine person who was not truly human, but merely took on a human appearance. Others claimed that Christ was truly human, but that his human nature was separate and distinct from his divine nature. This would mean that only his divine nature was the Son of God, while his human nature was the son of Mary. The effect of this was to make him not one but two persons. It would also mean that Mary would not be the mother of God, but only the mother of the man Jesus. To settle these disputes, an ecumenical council was held at Chalcedon (in present-day Turkey) in the year 451. Pope Leo the Great sent a letter to the council explaining his teaching on the nature of Christ: that Christ was one person with two natures – human and divine. The council accepted this teaching, and it has been the Church's official teaching about Christ ever since.

In his statement of belief, Pope Leo gives many examples of the presence of two natures – human and divine – in the one person of Christ. He is divine because he is the "Word of God," existing with the Father from eternity; he is human because "the Word was made flesh." He is human because he was born of a woman; divine because the woman was a virgin. As a human baby, he was wrapped in swaddling clothes and laid in a manger; as God, the child is worshipped by the Magi. As man, he was tempted by the devil; as God, when the temptation was over, "angels came and ministered to him" (Matthew 4:11). As man, he was hungry and thirsty; as God, he fed five thousand people with five loaves and two fish. As man, he wept when his friend Lazarus died; as God, he raised Lazarus to life again. As man, he suffered death through crucifixion; as God, he granted paradise to the "good thief" as he hung on the cross. As man, he said, "The Father is greater than I" (John 14:28); as God, he said, "I and the Father are one" (John 10:30).

There is yet another title that is added to Jesus' name. We refer to him as Jesus Christ *Our Lord*. What do we mean when we call Christ "Our Lord"? We have already seen that Jesus as the Christ or "the anointed one" is both a priest and a king. In the gospels, Jesus is depicted as a very misunderstood person. I suppose we could say that this was another indication of his humanity. We all know how it feels to be misunderstood. When this happens, it is often because other people expect us to be something or someone we are not. They misunderstand because we do not live up to what they expect of us. Think of a father who is pushing his son or daughter to become a doctor. But he or she has no interest in or aptitude for being a doctor, and wants to be a writer. The father misunderstands.

· This is what happened to Christ. He was misunderstood because some people wanted him to be something he was not. His fellow Jews were living under the domination of the Romans, since their country had become part of the Roman Empire. When Jesus appeared, many recognized him as the promised Messiah who would free them and save them. Some of them, however, believed that this meant being saved and freed from the Romans. They wanted Jesus to liberate them from Roman rule, so they could become an independent kingdom once again. But Jesus had no intention of setting up that kind of kingdom. As "the anointed one" – a priest and a king – Christ did want to establish a kingdom, but his kingdom was to be a *spiritual* one. We need to understand what kind of kingdom Christ has and what we mean when we call him "Lord" of that kingdom.

When Christ stood on trial before Pontius Pilate, Pilate asked him if he claimed to be the "king of the Jews." Christ did not deny his kingship but said, "My kingship is not of this world." He then explained that if he were trying to set up a worldly kingdom, his followers would be fighting to prevent his being arrested and convicted. Then he explained his mission: "For this I was born and for this I have come into the world, to bear witness to the truth" (John 18:33-37). Christ did not come into the world to exercise political or military power. He came to tell us the truth about God, about God's love for us and about how we should live as children of God. Those who accept the truth that Christ proclaimed to the world, and try to live according to that truth, are accepting Christ as Lord. They become members of the kingdom he rules – a kingdom in which he wants to unite all human beings.

What kind of a kingdom is the kingdom of Christ? A special feast to honour Christ as king is celebrated on the last Sunday of the Church's liturgical year. In the prayer that introduces the Eucharistic prayer at that feast, the priest calls to mind that Jesus Christ was anointed by his Father as both priest and king. As priest, "he offered his life on the altar of the cross and redeemed the human race." As king, "he claims dominion over all creation" and presents a kingdom to his Father. That kingdom is "eternal and universal," that is, Christ wants everyone to be part of this kingdom, and it will last forever. It will not eventually die, like the Roman Empire or the British Empire. It will last forever because it is not kept alive by military power or economic success or political wisdom. It is a kingdom of "truth and life," of "holiness and grace," and of "justice, love and peace." Wherever you find such things as truth, life, justice, love and peace, there you find the kingdom of

Christ in action. And it lasts forever because such things last forever. It is a spiritual kingdom because it lives by those things that are inspired by the Spirit of God. Christ wanted to create a kingdom where people live together in justice, love and peace. In the words of Pope Benedict XVI, it is a kingdom whose only power is "the power of truth and love."[4]

When we accept Christ as Lord, therefore, we are expressing a desire to be a member of this kingdom and to accept the responsibility to spread that kingdom and help it to grow. When we go to Mass, we believe that Christ is made sacramentally present on the altar. But Christ and his kingdom are also made present when Christians live as Christ their Lord wants them to live – when they live according to the truth that he proclaimed. Those who work for justice and peace in the world, those who minister to the poor and the sick, those who offer shelter to the homeless or feed the hungry – those, in other words, who practise the "works of mercy" – are making Christ's kingdom present in the world. But where does each one of us fit into this picture? How do we make ourselves a part of Christ's kingdom? I would say that whenever we try to understand and explain to others the truth that Christ proclaimed, we are promoting Christ's kingdom, which is a kingdom of truth. The same goes for any effort we make to acquire knowledge. Christ's kingdom is also made present whenever we try to help others and respond to their needs, for it is a kingdom of love; or when we fight for a just cause, for it is a kingdom

[4] Pope Benedict XVI, *St. Paul* (San Francisco: Ignatius Press, 2009), 69.

of justice; or when we are understanding and forgiving, for it is a kingdom of peace.

In ordinary human terms, the idea of serving someone as your "lord" means a loss of freedom. In ancient Rome, the lord or master would buy a slave from a slave dealer; the slave became his property. Slaves could be put to death if they tried to escape. In medieval times, the lord owned the land worked by the peasant farmer; peasants could keep only a portion of what they produced. Unlike this kind of lordship, the lordship of Christ does not take away the freedom of those who follow him. Christ does not *make* us serve him; we choose to do so. Those who truly live according to the truth that he preached – like the saints – are not enslaved but liberated. By becoming instruments or agents of Christ's love, forgiveness, compassion and generosity, they are liberated from their own selfishness, greed and pride. When some Jewish religious leaders asked Jesus when his kingdom would be established, he told them that his kingdom was not one that could be seen, could not be pointed to as being here or there (Luke 17:20-25). The kingdom of Christ is present wherever people serve Christ in this way that liberates them spiritually. And that means it is not in this or that place. It is all over the place.

Jesus Christ: Son of Mary

It was from Mary that Christ took his human nature. The special place that Mary has in the life and devotion of Christians is based on the fact that she – out of all the women in the world – was chosen to be the mother of Christ. And since the person to whom she gave birth was also divine, she is honoured with the title of "Mother of God." Devotion to Mary is particularly strong among Catholics. For this reason, the Church has tried to guide our thinking about Mary and her role in our salvation by formulating certain doctrines, such as the immaculate conception of Mary and the virginal conception of Jesus. The immaculate conception refers to the fact that since Mary was chosen to be the mother of the sinless Christ, she was born without that flaw in her nature that we call original sin. The virginal conception of Jesus (commonly referred to as the "virgin birth") means that Jesus was conceived in Mary's womb solely through the power of the Holy Spirit. Jesus did not have a human father; although she became a mother, Mary remained a virgin.

The fact that Christ is both God and man is a mystery and therefore is difficult to understand. The fact that Mary is both virgin and mother is also a mystery that is difficult to understand. But mysteries we cannot understand can still mean something to us. Christ's task was to reunite God and human beings by making it possible for us to become children of God. The fact that Christ combines a human nature and a divine nature in his own person demonstrates the kind of closeness he wanted to bring about between God and human beings. By the very fact of what he was, Christ taught us how close God wants to be to his people. In Christ we see God the Son becoming a human being and sharing every aspect of our human lives except sin. He was born just as we are, he went through all the stages of growing up, he suffered from fatigue and hunger and thirst, he was misunderstood and persecuted, and finally he suffered and died. The message seems to be that God wants to share and is interested in every aspect of our human lives. He is not some distant God thundering down at us from a mountain top. He is "Our Father." He cares about everything that happens to us just as our human fathers do.

There is, therefore, a meaning to Jesus' humanity. But does it really make any difference to us that Jesus' mother was a virgin? Like the idea of Christ being both God and man, the idea of Mary being both virgin and mother is a paradox – an apparent contradiction. A virgin gives birth to a child. Though we cannot understand this, it tells us something important: that God can make virginity fruitful and, therefore, valuable. If Christ told us something simply by what he was, so does Mary. She tells us that both virginity and motherhood are valid ways of serving God. Mary is a model for both ways of life. Her virginity also underlines the idea that a woman who remains unmarried – as a religious sister, a nun or a single woman in the world – can still become a "mother" to those she serves and cares for. When Mother Teresa died, she was mourned by all the people of India (which is a mostly non-Christian country) because they had lost the woman they called "mother." For them, she was truly a mother in the most loving and nurturing sense of that word. As a virgin who was also a mother, Mary is an inspiration to all women who bring loving care – who become "mothers" – to those in any kind of need. In Mary and in people like Mother Teresa, virginity becomes fruitful. That is the paradox.

If the ideas of a God–man and a virgin–mother are difficult to understand, so are the truths that Christ taught us, because they, too, are full of paradoxes. Christ taught us that those who embrace poverty voluntarily can find a different kind of wealth; that the humble will be exalted; that persecution and martyrdom can be seen as triumph and victory; that those who are simple often have the greatest wisdom. Christ and Mary in their very persons are living examples of the kind of paradoxical wisdom that it takes to be a Christian.

When we think of the Virgin Mary, I'm afraid we may be influenced by pictures and statues that project an overly sentimental and otherworldly image of her. We may forget what a strong woman she was and how she embraced the difficult life to which God called her. Mary has been presented to generations of Catholic girls and women as a model of purity and humility, and she is certainly that. But we must understand what lies behind Mary's purity and humility. If we see her as a model of purity simply because she was a virgin, we are missing a key part of the picture. Virginity does not make a person a saint. Mary was a virgin, but the Church has never seen virginity as an end in itself. It is a means to an end. It is the purpose behind a person's virginity that makes that person a saint. The purpose of Mary's – or anyone's – virginity is to leave oneself open to whatever God might ask one to do with one's life. If one's only desire is to go after what one wants and to be in complete control of one's own life, such a person can remain blind and deaf to what God wants. Mary's purity and humility enabled her to say *yes!* when God asked something of her. Her answer to the angel was "Let it be to me according to your word" (Luke 1:38).

Because of Mary's openness to what God wanted of her, God was able to do great things through her. Mary's reaction to God's call shows her humble attitude. After receiving the angel's message Mary went to visit her cousin Elizabeth. When Mary shared her news, she said, "He who is mighty has done great things for me" (Luke 1:49). In other words she gave God all the credit for what was happening. She did not consider herself as great, but rather as one who had received a great blessing from God. She did not say, "People from now on will call me 'Mary the Great.'" She said, "Henceforth all generations will call me *blessed*" (Luke 1:48). To be "blessed" literally means to have received a favour. Two thousand years later, that is exactly what we call her – *the Blessed Virgin*. Mary was blessed by God not simply because she was a virgin, but because her virginity was an expression of openness to what God wanted of her and for her. And what God wanted for her was a great blessing for her and for the whole world.

Sometimes we wonder how much of a role model Mary can be for women of the twenty-first century, whose situation is so different from hers. But perhaps we are overlooking some important aspects of Mary's personality. Mary is a model because of her strength of character – her "toughness." Think of the circumstances of Jesus' birth in a stable, of the forced exile in Egypt, and of having to watch her son die as a convicted criminal. Women today are expected to be strong and independent. I believe Mary measured up to that standard.

I am always struck by Mary's reaction to the event of Jesus' birth and the visit of the shepherds who told her about the vision of angels they had seen announcing Jesus' birth: "But Mary kept all these things, pondering them in her heart" (Luke 2:19). These words suggest that Mary was not just a blindly obedient and unthinking woman. She tried to think through and understand – she "pondered" – what God was doing in her life. She shows every sign of being a strong, thinking woman. And I am certain that in her thinking there were a lot of "whys." Why me? Why is this happening? Why is my son misunderstood? Why is he being put to death? Think about the strength Mary needed to stand by the cross and watch her son's execution, when most of his male followers had run away. When Mary said yes to God's plans for her, she said yes to a lot of pain and suffering. It reminds us that being "blessed" does not necessarily eliminate sorrow and suffering. Mary persevered in her response to God's call in spite of all these difficulties. There is a word for that. It is called *faith*.

Food for Thought

On the difference between the historical Jesus and the Christ of faith

To a large extent the only past events that are still accepted as valid are those that are presented as "historical," that is, tested and passed by historical methods. It is quite often forgotten that the full truth of history eludes documentary verification. ... So it must be said that historical science not only reveals but also conceals history. The automatic result is that it can see the man Jesus all right but it can only with difficulty discover the Christ in him, which as a truth of history cannot simply be checked as right or wrong by reference to the documentary evidence.

—Joseph Ratzinger (now Pope Benedict XVI) *Introduction to Christianity* (San Francisco: Ignatius Press, 2004), 196.

On the meaning of the Virgin Birth

The Old Testament contains a whole series of miraculous births, always at decisive turning points in the history of salvation ... and it reaches its climax and goal with Mary. The meaning of the occurrence is always the same: the salvation of the world does not come from man and from his own power; man must let it be bestowed upon him and he can only receive it as pure gift. The Virgin Birth is not a lesson in asceticism, nor does it belong directly to the doctrine of Jesus' Divine Sonship; it is first and last theology of grace, a proclamation of how salvation comes to *us*: in the simplicity of acceptance, as the voluntary gift of the love that redeems the world.

—Joseph Ratzinger (now Pope Benedict XVI) *Introduction to Christianity* (San Francisco: Ignatius Press, 2004), 277–278.

6

Salvation

Suffered under Pontius Pilate,
was crucified, died and was buried;
he descended into hell;
on the third day he rose again from the dead;
he ascended into heaven,
and is seated at the right hand
of God the Father almighty;
from there he will come to judge
the living and the dead.

What is salvation?

At first glance, the words of the opening two lines of the above passage from the Apostles' Creed seem unremarkable. They describe someone who was on trial before Pontius Pilate, the procurator of the Roman province of Judea, and who was condemned to death and then crucified. For Christians, however, these words are the heart and soul of our profession of belief, for they describe what we believe to be the events that brought about our salvation. These events reconciled us to or reunited us with God. They made it possible for us to become children of God and, as such, to inherit eternal life. Among these events, the Creed mentions Jesus' descent "into hell." The *Catechism of the Catholic Church* (#633) interprets the word "hell" in this passage as the "abode of the dead," similar in meaning to the Hebrew *Sheol* or the Greek *Hades*. In this sense, it refers to the dead who await the coming of Christ, their redeemer. In the meantime, their "hell" refers to the fact that they have been "deprived of the vision of God." It does not, therefore, have the same meaning as our current understanding of "hell," as an eternal loss of that vision of God. All these events refer to the deeper spiritual meaning behind the historical events. Before we consider the meaning of the salvation these words describe, it might be helpful to think about these events as *history*.

Pontius Pilate is one of only three human beings mentioned by name in the Creed, along with Jesus and Mary. We might well ask, Does he really belong in such company? Why would the Christians who composed the Creed include Pilate in describing the event of salvation? Clearly, they wanted to stress that Jesus' death on the cross really happened, that it was a real historical event. That is why they make it perfectly clear that it happened at a particular time or point in history. Pilate was the Roman procurator of Judea from 25 or 27 AD until 35 AD, so the Creed makes it clear that Jesus' crucifixion took place during that time span. We find the same concern for establishing the birth of Christ as a historical reality in the gospel of Luke, where we are told that Jesus' birth took place "when Quirinius was governor of Syria." Contrary to those who might claim that Jesus never existed or never died on the cross or never rose from the dead, Christians maintain that Christ was a real historical person whose death is reported not only in the gospels but by ancient writers such as the Jewish historian Josephus and the Roman historian Tacitus. The Creed also includes the resurrection in this recital of historical facts. The gospels point to the empty tomb and the witness of those who encountered the risen Christ to emphasize that the resurrection was a historical fact.

But why is all this important? Why is it important that our salvation be carried out by a real, historical human being, living in real historical time amid a series of real historical events? Why could not God have simply inspired a prophet to tell us that our sins were forgiven and that we were reconciled to God? Why was all the suffering, the death on the cross and a miraculous resurrection necessary? The beginning of an answer to these questions lies in the fact that our salvation is referred to as a process of "atonement." It is a process whereby we human beings who have been separated from God, are reconciled or reunited with God. In other words we are made to be "at one" with him: we can understand the word "atonement" as "at-one-ment." This work had to be accomplished by someone who was truly human and could therefore truly represent the human race. It was for this reason that God the Son, the second Person of the Trinity, became man. As both God and man, he reunited God and man – divinity and humanity – in his own person. The events we are discussing show that he was a real historical person who really shared our humanity. He suffered, just as we do. He died, just as we will. And his resurrection is a promise that we will rise from the dead, just as he did.

The question, however, remains: Exactly how does the death of Christ reunite us with God (atonement) and bring about our salvation? Christian thinkers have tried to answer this question in at least three different ways. These three answers are sometimes called "theories of atonement."

The first theory interprets Christ's saving death on the cross as bringing about some kind of liberation. This is called the *ransom theory*, because it sees Christ's death as the payment of a ransom to liberate us from enslavement to some alien power. We are liberated, for instance, from the power of Satan and adopted as children of God. Or the alien power may be thought of as sin, which we experience as an alien power controlling our lives and causing us to act against our better judgment. In the ransom theory, Christ's death is seen as the price or ransom paid to free us, just as someone might pay a ransom to free a person who has been kidnapped.

A second theory is called the *satisfaction theory*. This theory interprets the suffering and death of Christ as making satisfaction or paying a penalty for the sins of humanity that have offended God, and thereby reuniting or reconciling God and humanity. Christ is here seen as a sacrificial victim suffering for our sins.

A third theory is called the *moral influence theory*. In this theory, Christ is not a sacrificial victim but someone who reveals the goodness of God and gives us an example to follow. By identifying with Christ who identified himself with us, the image of God – which was lost due to sin – is restored in us.

The Church has not "canonized" any one of these theories – that is, made one of them official Church teaching. They are simply ways of imagining how Christ brought about our salvation. Each one might have a certain appeal to different types of people. Or theories like the ransom and satisfaction theories, in which Christ "pays a price" demanded by God for our redemption, may strike many people as making God out to be very harsh, demanding and even vengeful. It may not sound like the God they like to call "Our Father." And the moral influence theory gives us only an example to follow without explaining how salvation changes us and makes us capable of living as children of God. It is as if we have to do it all on our own. I suggest, therefore, that we rethink these ideas of salvation and look at it in a different way.

The word "salvation" literally means "healing." The word "salve," for instance, refers to a kind of healing ointment. The Latin word *salve*, which is a way of saying "hello," literally means "be well." To be saved therefore means to be healed or be well and I suggest that this is how we should experience salvation. To lapse into the question-and-answer mode of the old catechism, we might pose these two questions about salvation:

(1) Q. How does our salvation come about? A. By the grace of God."

(2) Q. From what are we saved? A. From sin.

If sin is what we are saved from and salvation means healing, then sin is the thing about us that has to be healed. That healing is accomplished by the grace of God. If we want to understand salvation, then, we need to understand these two words – sin and grace.

What is sin?

Did you ever feel that you were not being yourself? That instead of being true to yourself you were acting the way your friends or colleagues wanted you to act? That you were *conforming* to what others wanted you to be? Did you ever feel disappointed in yourself because you were not living up to your ideals? Have you ever been baffled by your own behaviour and said, "Why did I do that?" If you can answer "yes" to any or all of these questions, then you have had some experience of what the word "sin" means. I am not saying that any of these experiences are "sins," which are acts or omissions contrary to the moral law and your own conscience. I am talking about the "state" of sin in which we are born – what Christian tradition calls "original sin." The Adam and Eve story is a mythical way of telling us that as human beings we are *flawed*, and that this flaw in our human nature – the *state* of sin – is the root cause of the *actual sins* we commit. In saying that we "inherit" this state from our first parents, the myth is revealing that we *all* experience this flaw. We do so because we all do what

Adam and Eve did. Like them, we all "eat from the tree of
the knowledge of good and evil." In other words, we learn
the difference between good and evil, develop a conscience
and begin to experience guilt. This is the truth that the
mythical language of the story conveys.

And what exactly is that flaw in our human nature?
In Chapter 1, I mentioned the lifelong conflict between
the need to be ourselves – a unique "somebody" – and
the need to "fit in" and be part of a group. Sometimes the
need to belong, to be accepted, to conform to what others
expect of us is so strong that our real selves – the unique
somebody that makes us different from others – gets lost
in the shuffle. The role we are playing to please others takes
the place of the person we really are. We are not expressing our true selves, but are taking on the ideas, attitudes,
dress, language and even prejudices of others. We become
separated from our true selves. That is the fundamental
meaning of the state of sin. It is a state of *separation*. If we
create a false self in order to fit into a group, we experience a separation between our true self and that false self.
We feel divided within ourselves. And we are likely to feel
guilty about the whole thing, even if no "actual sin" has
been committed, because it indicates a lack of *integrity* on
our part. Integrity simply means being true to ourselves.
It means being the same person regardless of where we
are or who we are with. If we create a false self in addition
to our true self, we are no longer one person but two, and
are divided within ourselves. ("Integrity" comes from the
Latin *integer*, which means "one" or "whole.") We can feel

that same kind of separation when we fail to live up to our ideals and convictions. In this case, the separation is between the person we should be and want to be and the person we actually are. What we are separated from is our "better self."

To this point, we have considered only a kind of separation or dividedness that we experience within ourselves – separation from our true and better selves. We know very well, however, that there is another kind of separation – the separation that we experience between ourselves and other people. It reveals itself in some very common human experiences. Some examples might be: feeling lonely in a crowd; having a quarrel or misunderstanding with a good friend, spouse, children, parents or co-workers; enjoying another person's failure or embarrassment; putting another person down to feel superior; experiencing the hostility that is based on differences of race, religion or nationality. All are examples of a fundamental separation between individuals and groups and that can seem difficult to overcome. Becoming that unique somebody we were meant to be is important, but it also creates a barrier between us and others. It means we have become *different* from everyone else, but this in turn means we have become *separate* from everyone else. Getting to truly know others, communicating with others, working with others and loving others – all these must overcome that barrier of separation.

A third type of separation exists as well. We feel it when we wonder about the ultimate meaning and purpose of our lives. Does life mean anything beyond getting a job, getting promotions, paying off a mortgage and saving for retirement? Does life mean anything more than *getting*? Questions like these leave us feeling very limited in terms of knowledge and wisdom. They leave us feeling that the search for truth is endless. This is also a type of separation, because we feel separated from ultimate truth and from the ultimate meaning and purpose of our lives. A religious person experiences this state as separation from God, who is seen as the ultimate source of truth and meaning. We feel limited and *finite*, whereas God is unlimited and *infinite*.

We may, therefore, experience the state of sin or separation in three ways: from ourselves (our true and better selves), from others, and from God. When we commit an actual sin – that is, do something "sinful" – we are expressing the state of sin or separation in which we live, but we are also making that separation worse. If, for instance, I treat a friend badly, my conscience will eventually bother me. What will bother me is that I have separated myself (1) from God, because this is not the way a child of God should act; (2) from my friend, because I have injured our friendship; and (3) from myself, because I have acted contrary to my true and better self. To say that I am in need of "salvation" means that I want all these forms of separation to be healed. I want what is separated to be reunited. I want to feel closer to my true and better self, to other people, and to God. I want to be the person who, deep down, I believe myself to be. I want to feel a real solidarity with others. I want to feel as close to God as I do to my own father. In the Christian view, grace brings about this healing or reunion. We need to be "saved" from this state or condition of separation by the grace of God. If the whole world were to experience this kind of threefold healing, we would have some idea of what the "kingdom of God" means.

What is grace?

In trying to understand the meaning of grace, let's begin with these words of St. Paul – words that we hear at the Christmas midnight Mass: "The grace of God has appeared, bringing salvation to all" (Titus 2:11). If these words are read at Mass at Christmas, then the Church must want to stress that with the birth of Christ, the grace of God has come into the world. It has "appeared" in the person of Christ. And what is this "grace" that has "appeared"? It is simply God's love for us human beings. This love is what appeared with the birth of Christ, and this love is intended to heal our state of separation from God, from others and from ourselves – the state of sin. We call God's love for us "grace" because it is given freely and unconditionally. It is a gift that cannot be earned. It is given as a favour. (The Latin word for grace – *gratia* – can also be translated as "favour.") God does not love us because we deserve it or have earned it. God loves us simply because we are his. This is the heart and soul of the Christian message of salvation. What is revealed in the life, death and resurrection of Christ is God's unconditional love for all of us, without exception. It is a love we do not earn by observing laws and performing rituals – there are other reasons for those things. It is a love we simply believe in and respond to with faith. As mentioned in Chapter 2, that response of faith means to have a *trusting* belief in what God has revealed to us in Christ (his love) and what he has promised us in Christ (eternal life).

At Christmas we celebrate the birth of Christ because Christmas means that God's grace – God's love – has "appeared" in the person of Christ. This is the meaning of and the reason for the Christmas celebration. We are celebrating the fact that God's love has been revealed not just in words, but in a person. That person expresses God's love for us in a *human* way so we can understand and appreciate it. To have faith means to believe in the love of God as it is revealed in Christ, just as a husband and wife, for instance, believe in – have a trusting faith in – each other's love. It would be a mistake for them to think they have earned or deserve each other's love. Their love is not earned; it is a gift they give each other. In fact, it is impossible to earn anyone's love. We can earn respect and admiration, but we cannot earn anyone's love. Love either happens or it doesn't happen; when it happens, it is a *gift*. It is given freely, not as something owed. What is revealed in the person of Christ is that this is the way God loves us – with a love that is a gift because we cannot earn or deserve it. And, as the crucifix reminds us, Christ loves us to the point of death.

The crucifix is a symbol of God's grace, God's love for us. It reminds us of two important qualities of genuine love. First, love expresses itself in self-sacrifice for the sake of the one you love. Second, love expresses itself in compassion, and Christ's death on the cross was the ultimate expression of compassion. "Compassion" literally means to suffer with someone. Christ did this by becoming human and sharing every aspect of our human lives, with all the suffering that goes with being human. This included the suffering of death. To prove the extent of God's love, he chose the worst possible kind of death – being crucified as a condemned and disgraced criminal. In Christ, we discover that God loves us regardless of what kind of life we live. It is the love of a father for his children. God's love for us is the one constant thing in the life of a Christian. It is always there, even when we turn away from it.

At this point, the question that might arise is this: If God is going to love me anyway – regardless of the kind of life I live – what is the point of trying to live a good Christian life? Surely I can do anything I want and God will still love me. This age-old question is based on the false premise that the purpose of a good Christian life is to earn or be worthy of God's love and acceptance. The Christian life is not a matter of earning something from God by strenuous moral living and religious practices. It is, rather, a loving and grateful response to something (God's love) that has already been given. Moreover, though the question seems logical on the surface, it does not correspond to real life. (Logic does not always explain life.) If I am loved by someone whose love I value, the normal human response is not to see that love as something to take advantage of in an egocentric way – "he/she will love me anyway" – but rather to respond to it by loving the other in return. In fact, it is by being loved that we are rendered capable of loving.

The healing effect of love is a common human experience. The love of God is meant to have a healing effect on the forms of separation that afflict human existence. It is God's freely given love and my response of faith that bring me into a closer, father-child relationship with God and overcome my separation from God. It also helps to overcome my separation from others, because I recognize that those others are also objects of God's love. It also has a healing effect on my inner separation from my true and better self through God's loving acceptance of my divided and imperfect self. It allows me to face and accept myself in that separated state. That self-acceptance is the first step towards overcoming my inner separation. In other words, salvation is taking place, if only in a partial and incomplete sense in this life.

The mystery of salvation

Earlier in this chapter I asked a question: Why was the suffering and death and resurrection of Christ necessary? The answer I suggested was that these events make up the *event* of salvation, and that salvation had to be accomplished by a real, historical human being who could truly represent the human race. Now I want to suggest another reason why all this happened. These events took place because the death and resurrection of Christ demonstrate the pattern of our own salvation. We too, through the grace of God, "die" and "rise" to a new life. That new life in Christ is grounded in the assurance of God's love and acceptance of us that is revealed in the person of Christ who loved us to the point of death.

The cross is a powerful symbol. We can think of it this way. Its vertical beam represents the reuniting of heaven and earth, God and humanity. Its horizontal beam – with Christ's arms stretched out on it as if to embrace the whole world – represents the reuniting of human beings with one another, since they are all objects of the same love or grace. The cross represents the healing of separation and, therefore, represents grace. It also reminds us that love is expressed by sacrifice.

In Chapter 3, we explored the word "mystery." Mystery can refer to something puzzling or difficult to figure out. But it can also refer to a visible object or ritual or event that is a sign of a deeper, invisible, spiritual reality or event. In this sense, the death and resurrection of Christ is a mystery – a visible sign of our own "death" to sin and our rising to the new life of grace and faith. This is the spiritual effect of Christ's visible death and resurrection. That is why we often hear the phrase "the *mystery* of our salvation." This mystery is sometimes called the Easter mystery or Paschal mystery. Passover is a Jewish feast that celebrates the historical event of the escape of the Israelites from slavery in Egypt under the leadership of Moses. It also represents their spiritual transformation from slavery to freedom. In its celebration of the Paschal mystery at Easter, the Church links three historical experiences, giving similar meaning to each. These experiences are (1) the Passover experience of the Israelites when they passed from slavery to freedom in their exodus from Egypt; (2) the Passover experience of Christ in his death and resurrection, as he passed from death to life; and (3) the Passover experience of the Christian who, in baptism, also passes from slavery and death (sin) to freedom and life (grace). What the term "Paschal mystery suggests is that the Passover experience of the Jews prefigures or foretells the Passover experienced by Christ in his death and resurrection. And that experience of Christ is the pattern for the spiritual Passover experience of the Christian.

How are these three series of events connected?

(1) Every year, Jews celebrate the feast of Passover to commemorate the great event of liberation in their history – their escape from slavery in Egypt under the leadership of Moses. In the biblical story, the "angel of death" passed over the houses of the Jews and spared their firstborn children from death; then the Jews, in their escape, "passed over" from slavery to freedom (Exodus 12–14). Christ's death and resurrection was also a Passover, in the sense of passing from death to life. Through the grace of God and the response of faith, the Christian also passes from spiritual slavery and death to the freedom of life in Christ.

(2) Just before their escape from Egypt, God commanded the Israelites to offer a lamb in sacrifice and to eat the lamb – the "Paschal lamb" – in a special ritual meal. The Passover experience of Christ also contains a ritual meal (the Last Supper) and a sacrifice (the death of Christ on the cross). Christians see the sacrifice of the Paschal lamb as prefiguring the sacrifice of Christ. Like the Pascal lamb, Christ offered himself as a sacrifice for our salvation. At Mass we pray to him as the "Lamb of God" and

commemorate and re-enact in a sacramental way the Last Supper and the sacrifice of Christ on the cross.

(3) To achieve their freedom, the Israelites had to pass through the waters of the Red Sea. With that event they became the "People of God," called to a new life and a mission to preserve and bring to the world the worship of the one true God. Christ, in a similar way, passed through the waters of the Jordan River when he was baptized by John the Baptist. At that event, the voice of God was heard proclaiming Christ as God's Son and confirming his mission as humanity's saviour. The Christian, also, through the waters of baptism, is reborn to a new life, made a child of God, given a new calling or vocation to carry the spirit of God's love to the world, and made a member of the new "People of God" – the Church.

(4) The Passover of the Israelites from slavery to freedom was completed when they took possession of the land God had promised them. Christ's Passover was completed when he was glorified by rising from the dead and ascending into heaven where, as the Creed puts it, he is "seated at the right hand of God." The Passover of the Christian from the death of sin to the life of grace is completed by the gift of eternal life that God has promised.

What all this means is that the world's salvation was prefigured or foreshadowed in the events of the Jewish Passover, accomplished in the death and resurrection of Christ, and completed in the Christian experience of God's grace. The Creed also tells us that this same Christ will "come to judge the living and the dead." It is the Christ who proclaimed God's love for us who will judge the genuineness of our response of faith to that love.

Food for Thought

On the experience of sin as separation

I should like to suggest another word to you, not as a substitute for the word "sin" but as a useful clue in the interpretation of the word "sin": "separation." ... To be in the state of sin is to be in the state of separation. And separation is threefold: there is separation among individual lives, separation of man from himself, and separation of all men from the Ground of Being [God]. This threefold separation constitutes the state of everything that exists; it is a universal fact; it is the fate of every life. And it is our human fate in a very special sense. For *we* as men know that we are separated. ... We know that we are estranged from something to which we really belong, and with which we *should* be united. We know that the fate of separation is not merely a natural event like a flash of sudden lightning, but that it is an experience in which we actively participate, in which our whole personality is involved, and that, as fate, it is also *guilt*. Separation which is fate *and* guilt constitutes the meaning of the word "sin." ... *Existence is separation!* Before sin is an act, it is a state.

—Paul Tillich, *The Shaking of the Foundations* (New York: Scribner's Sons, 1948), 154–155.

On the experience of grace as reuniting what is separated

In the light of this grace we perceive the power of grace in our relation to others and to ourselves. ... We experience the grace of being able to accept the life of another, even if it be hostile and harmful to us, for, through grace, we know that it belongs to the same Ground [God] to which we belong and by which we have been accepted. We experience the grace which is able to overcome the tragic separation of the sexes, of the generations, of the nations, of the races, and even the utter strangeness between man and nature. Sometimes grace appears in all these separations to reunite us with those to whom we belong. For life belongs to life.

—Paul Tillich, *The Shaking of the Foundations* (New York: Scribner's Sons, 1948), 162.

On being a child of God

Adam, heeding the words of the serpent, wants to become God himself and to shed his need for God. We see that to be God's child is not a matter of dependency, but rather of standing in the relation of love that sustains man's existence and gives it meaning and grandeur.

From Pope Benedict XVI, *Jesus of Nazareth* (New York, Doubleday, 2007), 138–139.

7

The Christian Community

I believe in the Holy Spirit,
the holy catholic Church,
the communion of saints,
the forgiveness of sins,
the resurrection of the body,
and life everlasting.

In Chapter 3, we saw that the Creed can be divided into three parts, corresponding to the three Persons of the Trinity. Part 1 states what we believe about God the Father as our creator. Part 2 states what we believe about God the Son as our saviour. Part 3 states what we believe about the Holy Spirit as our sanctifier. In this third part of the Creed, we begin by proclaiming our belief in the Holy Spirit, but this is followed by a statement of our belief in the Church, the communion of saints, the forgiveness of sins and, finally, our belief in God's promise of resurrection and eternal life. All these beliefs refer to the process of our sanctification, which begins with our baptism, when we receive the gift of the Holy Spirit, and achieves its goal when we attain eternal life. This section of the Creed, then, is about the Holy Spirit, because it is about our sanctification, which is the work of the Holy Spirit. It is important to understand what we are saying in each part of this section and how it relates to the sanctification of the Christian community.

I believe in the Holy Spirit

Belief in the Holy Spirit means at least three things.

(1) *We believe that the Holy Spirit exists as the third Person of the Trinity.* I have suggested that a human way of thinking about the mystery of the Trinity is to think of God the Son as the Father's idea of himself, which is so perfect an image of the Father that it is another Person. And the relationship of love between these two Persons is so perfect that it also is another Person. The Holy Spirit, then, is the love or the bond between the Father and the Son.

(2) *We believe in the presence of the Holy Spirit in the Church.* After Jesus' ascension into heaven, the apostles, with Mary and some women who had followed Jesus, gathered in the "upper room" to pray and await the Holy Spirit whom Christ had promised. This gathering was the first Christian community – the beginning of the Church. After nine days, the Holy Spirit descended on them in the visible form of "tongues as of fire"(Acts 2:3). Ever since then, Christians have believed that the Holy Spirit is present in the Church as Christ promised he would be. The work of the Church is twofold: it must preach the Christian message to the world and it must help its members to respond to that message through its preaching, the sacraments, and

the doctrinal and moral guidance it gives them. Christians believe that the Holy Spirit is present in the Church to help it carry out this twofold task.

(3) *We believe that each of us receives the Holy Spirit, especially in baptism and confirmation.* This should remind us that the Holy Spirit is given to the whole Church: not just to its leaders – the pope and the bishops – but to every member of the Church. Why is the Holy Spirit given to us? For our sanctification. The word "sanctify" literally means to "make holy." If we think for a moment about who the Holy Spirit is, we can perhaps understand what being "sanctified" or made holy means. If the Holy Spirit is the relationship of love between the Father and the Son, then to receive the Holy Spirit means to be given a share in that relationship. In other words, to be sanctified by the Holy Spirit means to be made a child of God – to share in the Son's relationship with the Father. As St. Paul puts it, "All who are led by the Spirit of God are sons of God" (Romans 8:14). To receive the Holy Spirit means to be sanctified by being raised to a holy or sacred status as a child of God.

Why is it important for us to think of ourselves as children of God? Because it reminds us of the kind of relationship we have with God through the gift of the Holy Spirit. It reminds us that it is like the relationship of children to their parents, which is a very personal kind of relationship. We need to remember this because many Christians seem to think that their relationship to God is some kind of legal relationship. They see God as a lawgiver whose laws we must obey to earn God's love and acceptance.

But we do not earn God's love by our own human efforts. (This way of thinking was condemned by the Church in the fifth century.) God's love is a gift, and that gift is the Holy Spirit, who is the love of God (the love between the Father and the Son). Again, as St. Paul put it, "God's love has been poured into our hearts through the Holy Spirit who has been given to us" (Romans 5:5). Through the gift of that love, we become children of God; our relationship with God is that of a child to a parent, not that of a subject to a lawgiver. It is personal, not legal.

What is the difference between a legal relationship and a personal one? A legal relationship is governed by laws or rules that tell us exactly what we must do or not do: for example, the exact speed limit to observe, the exact amount of taxes to pay, exactly what is allowed or forbidden. Such laws are necessary, but if we reduce our Christian life to this kind of exact rule keeping, it can give us a false sense of security and make us feel smug. It can make us feel that we have earned a reward from God because we have "kept all the rules." What Christ thought about this kind of smug self-satisfaction is made clear in the parable of the Pharisee and the Publican (Luke 18:9-14).

Of course, our relationship with God is not this kind of legal relationship of laws and rules. If as children of God our relationship with God is like the relationship of a child to a parent, it includes rules (commandments); but it would be foolish to say that those rules are the only thing that governs the child-parent relationship or the only thing that holds child and parent together. Clearly, there is much more going on between them: the love they have for each other, the experiences they have shared, and the simple fact that they "belong" to each other. In other words, they are held together not by a set of rules but by a certain "spirit" that adds up to a lot more than rules. The physical and emotional bond makes parents want to do more than impose rules and makes children want to do more than obey rules. Rules cannot exhaust the meaning or convey the reality of the parent-child relationship. The same goes for our relationship with God. It is based not on rules alone but, as with a parent and child, on a certain "spirit," the Holy Spirit, that bonds and unites.

As children of God, we are to live according to the Spirit who has been given to us. St. Paul offers two guidelines for living a Christian life – that is, living as a child of God.

(1) *Live according to the Spirit and not according to the "flesh"* (Galatians 5:16-24). Living according to the Spirit obviously refers to the Spirit (God's love) that has been given to us and that makes us children of God. But what does it mean to live "according to the flesh"? Many people seem to think it refers only to forms of physical self-indulgence, such as sexual immorality, gluttony and drunkenness. But when St. Paul lists the "works of the flesh," he also includes things like "enmity, jealousy, anger, selfishness, dissension and envy." These are all expressions of egoism or selfishness. Things like "impurity, licentiousness and drunkenness" are included because, like the others, they are expressions of egoism. So the real "sin of the flesh" – the opposite of "living according to the Spirit" – is living

a life of egoism, selfishness and self-indulgence. Living by the Spirit of God's love, on the other hand, means a life of selfless love of others. When St. Paul lists the "fruits of the Spirit" – the expressions of this kind of selflessness – he mentions "love, joy, peace, patience, kindness, gentleness, self-control." These are the expressions of a selfless love of others – the opposite of egoism. We do not need detailed and minute laws or rules to practise them; they are simply the way we treat the people we love.

(2) *Live according to the Spirit and not according to the letter of the law.* When we live according to the letter of the law, we reduce what God expects of us to exact obedience to a set of rules. This leads to all kinds of hair-splitting over what exactly the rules demand and how far we can go before the rule is broken – not to mention all the anxiety over whether we are in the "state of grace." Again, we have reduced our relationship with God to a legal arrangement rather than a personal bond. Living by the letter means living by the rules of a legal relationship rather than the spirit of a personal relationship. It means turning something that should be joyful into a deadly burden. And yet Christ said, "My yoke is easy and my burden is light" (Matthew 11:30). St. Paul tells us that with the coming of Christ, a "new covenant" – a new kind of relationship – was inaugurated between God and us. In this new relationship, we serve God "not in a written code but in the Spirit; for the written code kills but the Spirit gives life" (2 Corinthians 3:6). When we feel that we are genuinely loved by others simply for who we are and not for what we do, we are freed from the

burden of proving ourselves worthy and from the anxiety and self-absorption that go with that burden. This in turn means we are free to love and be concerned about other people. The gift of God's love – the Holy Spirit – is meant to have the same effect. It is supposed to liberate us from ourselves so we can love others. Loving others, then, is not just a commandment. It is something that the gift of the Holy Spirit makes possible. Freedom from concern about ourselves means freedom to love and be concerned about others. As Pope Benedict XVI explains in his encyclical letter *Deus est Caritas*, "Love can be 'commanded' because it has first been given" (#14).

I believe in the holy catholic Church

What do we mean when we say that we "believe in" the Church? Surely it is not the same thing as "believing in" God. Believing in God means we have a trusting belief in God's love and acceptance of us and in God's promise of eternal life. To believe in the Church means to believe that the Church is a community of faith created by God through the gift of the Holy Spirit. We also believe that through its preaching, teaching and sacraments, the Church offers us the means of sanctification – the help we need to live as children of God. So the Church is not the object of our faith – God is: but our belief in the Church expresses our conviction that we were not meant simply to have a one-on-one relationship with God. We were meant to be part of a community of faith and love. This is the community that believes in, celebrates and tries to respond to Christ's message of salvation. We are not called to simply save our own souls; we are called to be members of a community – a Church.

I have suggested that the gift of the Holy Spirit, the freely given gift of God's grace or love, is meant to make it possible for Christians to stop worrying about and therefore being preoccupied with themselves. This makes possible the kind of self-transcendence – a rising above or growing beyond self-preoccupation – that in turn makes it possible to love others. This gift of God's love and the resulting care and concern for others rather than ourselves makes community possible. And that is what the Church is – a community created by the Holy Spirit. Sometimes when people talk about "the Church," they are talking about the structured institution: the pope, bishops and clergy, who form the "chain of command" that governs the Church. Every community, of course, must structure itself by having officers to govern and lead. But the Church as a community includes all of us. The leaders of that community have only one function: to help all its members to live Christian lives, to thereby create a loving community and to help the world to do likewise. Let's look at the main ways in which the Church helps its members to live a Christian life.

(1) *Through its preaching and teaching.* St. Augustine said, "I believe in order to understand and I understand in order to believe." I believe Augustine meant that he would never properly understand the faith unless he approached it with an attitude of faith. On the other hand, his faith would never be genuine unless he understood it properly.

All Christians could make the same statement. Our faith will never have meaning for our lives unless we constantly strive to deepen our understanding of it. This is why a large portion of the Church's task is educational. It must explain the faith to its members. This includes everything from the homily at Sunday mass to educational programs in parishes, schools, universities and elsewhere, since truth of every kind leads to God, who is truth itself.

(2) *Through its sacramental life*. A sacrament is a "visible sign of grace." That is why it is sometimes called a "mystery" – a visible, tangible, external sign of some invisible spiritual reality. As already mentioned, theologians sometimes speak of Christ as the "sacrament" of God because Christ is God become visible in a human form. In his visible humanity, Christ reveals the presence of the invisible God. And if Christ reveals the presence of God, then the sacraments reveal the ongoing presence of Christ and his saving work in the Church. In the sacraments, Christ continues to make us children of God (baptism), strengthen us to live as children of God (confirmation), forgive our sins (reconciliation), renew and unite us to his redeeming sacrifice (Eucharist), call some to share his priesthood (holy orders) and others to serve him in the married state (matrimony), and strengthen the sick and dying (anointing of the sick). In the outward, material signs of the sacraments (water, oil, bread, wine, etc.), Catholics believe that the love of Christ for us is made truly present and effective.

(3) *Through its moral and spiritual guidance.* It is easy enough to say that we should respond to the gift of the Holy Spirit by living as children of God, but what does this mean? How do children of God express their love of God and love of fellow human beings in everyday life? How do they make right moral decisions in particular circumstances? It goes without saying that we should always follow what our conscience tells us to do or not to do. The *Catechism of the Catholic Church* states that "a human being must always obey the certain judgment of his conscience" (#1790). Freedom of conscience, however, does not mean doing whatever we feel like doing. It presupposes that we are sincerely trying to do the objectively right thing. In its moral teachings, the Church tries to determine what is objectively good or evil and to apply that knowledge to our particular circumstances. In those circumstances we make our own moral decisions, but with the help of the Church's moral guidance. That guidance makes sense only to those who are truly committed to living a Christian life. If that commitment is present, we will look to those teachings for guidance. If there is no such commitment, those teachings will be seen as a burden. Morality will become obedience to someone else's rules of what is "allowed" or "not allowed." And that is the morality of a five-year-old. If, on the other hand, we can internalize the moral beliefs and values of the Church and thereby make them our own moral values, then we will not simply be blindly obeying someone else's rules but being true to our own values. In this way, the motivation for our moral lives comes from *within us*, which means our moral decisions are free decisions.

The communion of saints

As mentioned above, some people see only the external reality of the Church. They see a structured organization governed by rules, a kind of club. To belong to the club, you must follow the rules. To think this way is to miss the point. While the Church is certainly a visible society with structure, organization and a chain of command, it is much more. It is a spiritual community that is held together not simply by its visible organization but by the spiritual, invisible reality of God's grace. It is not just a society but a community, or – better still – a *communion*. It is a communion of all those who, through baptism, have received the grace of God – the love of God in the form of the Holy Spirit – and have thereby become children of God. It is that love, that Spirit, that holds the Church together and creates a true communion. When we receive communion at Mass, we are participating in a sacrament that is a visible sign not only of our invisible union with Christ, but of the invisible spiritual communion that unites all of us in one Church – the one "body of Christ."

Because the Church is such a communion, the Creed expresses our belief in it as the "communion of saints." The word "saints" does not suggest that we are claiming any personal saintliness for ourselves. We are claiming that we have been "sanctified"; we have been given a holy or sacred status as children of God by the gift of the Holy Spirit. This means that the communion of saints includes not only the members of the Church in this world, but also those in heaven, who have received their inheritance as children of

God, and those in purgatory, who are preparing to receive that inheritance.

The forgiveness of sins

As discussed in chapter six, the *state of sin* is that state of separation we experience from ourselves, from other people and from God. Things like selfishness, envy, anger and hatefulness remind us not only of our state of separation from and lack of solidarity with other people, but also of our estrangement from ourselves (our true and better selves) and of our estrangement from God, whose children we are and who wants us to live as such. They are expressions of that state of separation (sin) and tend to make that separation worse. Grace is the remedy for sin because the grace or love of God reunites what has been separated. Now, if the grace of God means God's love, then we can speak of the grace of forgiveness, because love is always forgiving. When we say, then, that we believe in the "forgiveness of sins," we are professing our belief in the forgiving quality of God's love.

How is God's forgiving love or grace received? If a sacrament is a visible sign of grace – of God's love – then it is not surprising that a special sacrament celebrates the forgiving quality of God's grace or love. This is the sacrament of reconciliation. In this sacrament, the love with which Christ forgave sinners is made present and effective in our lives, just as his redeeming sacrifice is made present in the Eucharist. This is important to remember because it is the love and forgiveness that God revealed in Christ that we receive. It is not the priest who forgives; he is simply the minister of God's forgiving grace. When Christ expressed his love for us by dying on the cross, he also expressed God's forgiveness of our sins. The forgiveness of sins, then, was accomplished once and for all by Christ's redeeming sacrifice on the cross. When we confess our sins to a priest, we are celebrating and renewing our faith in the forgiveness that comes from God.

One last question: If it is God who forgives sin, why confess to a priest? It is true that one can confess directly to God, but there is something reassuring about hearing a human voice offering you forgiveness and encouragement. (Think of those who heard words of forgiveness from Christ himself.) This is the thinking behind the whole sacramental system. Sacraments are visible signs of the continuing presence of God's love and forgiveness. In this particular sacrament, it is the voice and gestures of the priest that make God's forgiving love present. The priest expresses God's forgiveness in a human way, just as Christ did. Another point to remember is that sin weakens our connection with the spiritual communion of the Church. In this sacrament, the priest restores the penitent to full communion with the other members of the Church. The term "reconciliation" is an apt name for this sacrament, since it emphasizes the understanding of sin as separation and the reconciling function of the sacrament as the healing of that separation.

The resurrection of the body and life everlasting

The *Catechism of the Catholic Church* states, "By death the soul is separated from the body, but in the resurrection

God will give incorruptible life to our body, transformed by reunion with our soul. Just as Christ is risen and lives forever, so all of us will rise at the last day" (#1016). Why does the Creed make such a point of the resurrection of the body? Here are some points to keep in mind.

(1) As mentioned in Chapter 6, our salvation is a transformation from sin to grace and follows the pattern of Christ's Passover from death to life. When Christ rose from the dead, he did so with a real but incorruptible body. Christians believe they will do likewise. The Christian martyrs, for instance, allowed their bodies to be killed not because they were disposable, and only their immortal souls mattered. They did so because they firmly believed that those same bodies would be resurrected incorruptible. Christ's resurrection was the basis for that belief.

(2) It is not just our souls that receive the gift of grace and salvation. We are redeemed as persons, and a human person has a body and soul. We are therefore redeemed, body and soul. We are children of God, body and soul. We receive the gift of the Holy Spirit, body and soul. We live our Christian life, body and soul. And the reward of eternal life is given to both body and soul.

(3) We could not live our Christian lives without our bodies. We could not serve God or our fellow human beings without our bodies. We need our bodies to express our love and concern for others. If only the soul were rewarded with eternal life, it would be like rewarding good intentions but not the carrying out of those intentions; like rewarding feelings but not the expression of those feelings; like rewarding love but not loving actions.

(4) Historically, the Church has always rejected any interpretation of Christianity or any kind of false asceticism that would involve a rejection of the body and its sexuality and the material world in general as evil. In the early centuries, for instance, the heretical group known as the Gnostics taught that salvation meant the soul's escape from the body and from the material world. The Church, on the other hand, taught that God sanctified the human body by becoming a human being with a human body, and that the body is the temple of the Holy Spirit and is destined for eternal life.

If the resurrected body is incorruptible, that is because it is destined for eternal life. This raises a question: What is eternal life? How can we describe the life of heaven? I believe St. Paul gives us a hint. In his First Letter to the Corinthians, Paul quotes the Old Testament prophet Isaiah: "No eye has seen nor ear heard, nor the heart of man conceived what God has prepared for those who love him." Then he adds that what no eye has seen, etc., "God has revealed to us through the Spirit" (1 Corinthians 2:9-10). What Paul seems to be saying is that God, through the gift of the Holy Spirit, has given us some idea of what eternal life might be. Paul's meaning might be obscure, but it is fair to read his words as referring to the fact that the life of faith and love that we live as a result of the gift of the Holy Spirit gives us some understanding of the life of heaven. Eternal life is not something that begins only after death; it is the ultimate perfection and fulfillment of the life of faith and love that we are living now.

To understand this idea, it is helpful to recall that the experience of God's grace and our response of faith are meant to change or transform us. By accepting God's love and acceptance as a free gift – that is, by simply believing in it – we are relieved of the burden of earning that love or justifying ourselves before God. As previously mentioned, we are liberated from self-absorption or preoccupation with ourselves and are more able to love and be concerned about others. Because we are loved, we can love others, and this is what creates the loving community that the Church is supposed to be. Since all of this is the work of the Holy Spirit, I believe it is fair to say that the Holy Spirit teaches us that eternal life is the perfection of the life of a loving community, freed from all the egoism that makes community life imperfect in this life. We should not think of heaven as a reward given to individuals for their virtuous lives. Eternal life or the "fullness of life" is not something individual but something we enjoy in communion with others.

Is this not also true in our ordinary human lives? When do we feel most alive? What circumstances make us feel alive? I believe the answer would be such experiences as being in love; experiencing the warmth of friendship; being part of a loving family circle; being free of enmity and discord in our lives; feeling that we are a vital part of a living community and making a contribution to that community. In these experiences we come to realize that life is not something that we experience as isolated individuals but only in relation to others and to the world. Even the inner life of God is the life of the love and relatedness of a Trinity of

Persons. There is a vital connection between life and love. The very word "existence" is derived from the Latin words *ex* and *sistere*, which, when combined, mean to "stand out." To exist, then, means to stand out towards the world and other people. Eternal life, like grace, is not something that can be earned; it is something hoped for as a result of a life of faith and love. People in love who describe that state as "heaven" or "heavenly" might be exaggerating, but they are also expressing a truth, because that is what heaven is – the perfection of the love that holds people together. On the other hand, people who are totally alone and isolated and who describe their lives as "hell" would also be expressing a truth, because that is what hell is. It is total separation and isolation – the opposite of heaven. Eternal life would appear to be the perfection of that love that binds people together and, therefore, a communal experience.

Food for Thought

On immortality

It is not, I think, from the noumenal point of view [the soul] that the indestructibility of the loved one can be affirmed: the indestructibility is much more that of a bond than of an object [the soul]. The prophetic assurance [of immortality] might be expressed fairly enough as follows: whatever changes may occur in what I see before me, you and I will persist as one: the event that has occurred and which belongs to the order of accident, cannot nullify the promise of eternity which is enclosed in our love, in our mutual pledge. … What is really important, in fact, is the destiny of that living link, and not that of an entity which is isolated and closed in on itself.

—Gabriel Marcel (French philosopher and dramatist, 1889–1973), *The Mystery of Being*. Vol. 2: *Faith and Reality* (Chicago: Regnery, 1960), 172–174.

On the meaning of the "communion of saints"

It's a very odd thing, but if you had asked St. Paul what he meant by the "Communion of Saints," I think he would have said, without much hesitation, "I mean that when one set of Christians is hard up, another set of Christians, in a different part of the world, sends round the hat and takes up a collection for them."

That principle of give and take between Christians is a very good illustration of what *we* mean by the Communion of Saints. The Church is divided into three large bits; part of it is on earth, part of it is in heaven, part of it is in Purgatory. The Church in heaven is All Saints. The Church in Purgatory is All Souls. The Church on earth is all sorts. We on earth are poorer than the saints in heaven, so we ask them to give us something. But we on earth are richer than the souls in Purgatory, so they ask us to give them something. It's the same old principle St. Paul used to preach, of give and take between Christians all round.

—Father Ronald Knox, *The Creed in Slow Motion* (New York: Sheed and Ward, 1949), 197.

Postscript

This brief excursion through the articles of the Apostles' Creed began with the assertion that the words of the Creed say something *to us* and something *about us.* I have suggested that it is only by understanding what the Creed says about us that each of us can truly recite it with faith and conviction – that is, as a statement of our *personal* beliefs. When each of us "personalizes" the Creed in this way, it becomes a statement of what we personally believe and stand for – a statement not just of Christian beliefs, but of our personal and Christian identity. That Christian identity might be expressed in the following declarations:

1) I am a creature of the God who is the "creator of heaven and earth." This means that God is what is ultimate and absolute in my life. God is the ultimate source of everything in my life that is good, true and beautiful. I am someone for whom God is the ultimate point of reference for everything in my life and, therefore, the absolute value against which every other value is measured. Everything in my life derives its value from how it relates to that supreme value.

2) I am someone for whom God the Son, the second Person of the Trinity, shared my humanity by becoming a human being. The Word of God "became flesh" in order to reveal God's love for me in a human way. In the humanity of this God become man, who suffered and died for my salvation, I find my Christian identity and an image of what it means to be truly human. In the words of Pope Benedict XVI, "[Jesus] comes from God and he is God. But that is precisely what makes him – having assumed human nature – a bringer of true humanity."[5]

3) As a Christian, I am someone who has received the gift of God's love in the gift of the Holy Spirit. Since the Holy Spirit is the love between the Father and the Son, in receiving the Holy Spirit I share in the Son's relationship with the Father. I become a child of God. And, just as in human affairs, this love received as a gift creates in the recipient the capacity to love others. In Pope Benedict XVI's words, "Anyone who wishes to give love must also receive love as a gift."[6]

---

[5] Pope Benedict XVI, *Jesus of Nazareth* (New York: Doubleday, 2007), 334.

[6] Pope Benedict XVI, Encyclical Letter *Deus Caritas Est*, 2005, #7.